PRESBYTERIANS
PEOPLE OF THE MIDDLE WAY

For Adult Inquirers and New Members

PRESBYTERIANS
PEOPLE OF THE MIDDLE WAY

HARRY S. HASSALL

Illustrated by Pat McGeachy

PROVIDENCE HOUSE PUBLISHERS

Franklin, Tennessee

Printed in the United States of America

00   99   98   97   96   5   4   3   2   1

Library of Congress Card Catalog Number: 96–69313

ISBN: 1–881576–88–4

Outline of chapter entitled "Thinking Like a Presbyterian" from *Meet Your Church*, used by permission of Joseph M. Gettys, Clinton, South Carolina.

Permission is granted from the Office of the General Assembly, Presbyterian Church (U.S.A.) to use material from the following sources: *The Constitution of the Presbyterian Church (U.S.A.), Part I: Book of Confessions* and Part II: *Book of Order*.

The publisher wishes to thank Alan V. Shields for the generosity of his time and his editorial assistance.

This volume is designed to be used with *Presbyterians—People of the Middle Way: For Adult Inquirers and New Members, Teacher's Guide*. For ordering information, contact the publisher.

Published by
PROVIDENCE HOUSE PUBLISHERS
238 Seaboard Lane • Franklin, Tennessee 37067
800-321-5692

To my best friend, my wife of forty years,
Carolyn Carter Hassall, and
to our children,
Hal and Kelly, Kathryn and Mark,
who encouraged their dad to pursue his calling
at unusual hours and in diverse circumstances
in the several communities
where we lived and ministered.

Contents

Foreword

I believe that the manner in which people are brought into membership in a congregation is a major influence upon the seriousness and depth of the commitment that will follow their reception by the session.

Our Presbyterian Constitution mandates each session with the "responsibility for preparing those who would become members of the congregation" (G-5.0401). While the session is given the freedom to "determine whether this instruction shall be given before or after the public profession (of faith)" (G-5.0402b), every session is required to engage in such preparation with all who unite with each congregation by profession of faith, by reaffirmation of faith, or by transfer of certificate.

Casual entry into church membership is likely to result in casual relationships to the responsibilities of church membership. Current research on church membership patterns indicate that healthy churches are most likely to place high demands upon people at the point of entry.

While I have become acquainted with numerous effective programs for the preparation of inquirers and new members, I regard this program by Harry Hassall as one of the finest currently available. It grows out of four decades of faithful witness and ministry across the entire spectrum of our Presbyterian family. It blends profound theological and ecclesiological insights with a warm style of communication that brings the complexities of the faith and order of the Presbyterian Church (U.S.A.) within the reach of first-time inquirers and advanced disciples.

The course is user-friendly and flexible. Its six one-hour lessons can be presented in separate class sessions, or in any configuration desired, including a one weekend format, along with a luncheon.

The plan is pedagogically sound, combining substantive content through reading and lectures, and open interaction in group and personal dialogue and sharing. The *Student Text* becomes an invaluable resource for continuing use and reference. The material is designed to be taught one-on-one, in a small group, or in a larger group with equal effectiveness.

In bringing this text to us, Harry Hassall is making a profound contribution to our Presbyterian family at a time in our history when the quality and depth of our commitment to Jesus Christ and to His Church is of utmost importance.

While this course is designed for inquirers and new members, I would urge its study by sessions and active members as well. Here is a significant tool for renewal within our churches.

—Gary W. Demarest
former Associate Director for Evangelism, PC(USA), and
Interim Pastor, Geneva Presbyterian Church, Laguna Hills, California

Preface and Acknowledgments

My present title at Highland Park Presbyterian Church, Dallas, Texas, is Director of Presbyterian Ministries. This welcomed assignment gives me two major duties, both of which I immensely enjoy:

1. I am to invite, welcome, and teach inquirers and prospects about faith in Jesus Christ and membership in the Presbyterian Church (U.S.A.), of which this congregation is an integral part

2. I am to seek to inform all current church members as to the heritage, values, and workings of our Presbyterian system as we seek faithfully to witness as we move towards the year 2000 A.D.

This particular text is designed primarily to be used in a study course introducing new people to the Presbyterian Church. Secondarily, portions of this text may prove helpful to long-time Presbyterians as we seek to understand why Presbyterians act and respond to the issues of the day in certain almost predictable ways. A more careful investigation should reveal some of the competing values held by the Presbyterian mind-set which cause some to see things one way and others, just as faithful, to view things from an alternative perspective. Finally, it is my hope that all Presbyterians and friends of Presbyterians may seek to gain the long view of God's ways with humanity.

Not only does our generation need winsome evangelism, but we also desperately need the balance that a knowledge of origins and history tends to provide. Our conflicted generation with its life-and-death national debates needs that Gamalielian wisdom and confidence in the sovereignty of God that would enable Presbyterians to do all things "decently (that is, with civility) and in order (that is, within the agreed-upon rules)." Furthermore, we Presbyterians, who theologically insist on the doctrine of "total depravity," should not be too surprised when people (including other Presbyterians and ourselves) practice this doctrine. We, who proclaim the grace of God as a primary conviction, also would do well to emulate God's patience in our relationships with our fellow Presbyterians, even those who seem to "push the envelope" of our definition of what is Presbyterian.

The whole Presbyterian family needs such warm, inviting, gentle evangelism and such broad, caring, and forgiving understanding of who we are as a unique Presbyterian "people of the middle way" in God's universal economy. It is my goal to provide both of these where possible. Hopefully this book will expand the possibilities inherent in these concepts for others, either present Presbyterians or about-to-be Presbyterians. The five purposes of this text are as follows:

1. Gently to invite persons to faith in Jesus Christ

2. To encourage inquirers to become members of the Presbyterian family

3. To enable present Presbyterians to understand who we are by faith and by heritage through our position within the world Protestant movement

4. To enlist all to appreciate our heritage, our biblical convictions, and our commitment to the education of the head and to the compassion of the heart, in our search for equity, civility, and orderliness

5. To obtain the larger view of life by practicing confidence in the sovereignty of God

Over the years I have been a student of some of the great Presbyterians of the mid-twentieth century: C. Morton Hanna, Kenneth J. Foreman Sr., Ernest Trice Thompson, Ben Lacy Rose, Walter L. Lingle, Joseph M. Gettys, Stuart R. Oglesby, and J. Wayte Fulton Jr.— all of whom taught me not only the facts about Presbyterianism but also illustrated in their teaching and living the Presbyterian "ethos" or tone which is so essential to exhibit in our Presbyterian dealings with one another and the outside world. If nothing else is learned from this text, I would pray it would be the tone by which we Presbyterians seek to follow the Living God as revealed in Jesus Christ. Such a practice would alter our behavior, brighten our public image, and prove us more faithful to the Lord of the Church.

I am grateful for my parishioners, students, and friends over the years, who have heard me introduce Jesus Christ and who have participated in my teaching about the Presbyterian family. Some have indeed become Christians and Presbyterians, and many have sought to live the Christian life faithfully within the Presbyterian Church. These may be found in small congregations and in large. My message has frequently been taught in conversational dialogue in living rooms, as well as in meetings of confirmation classes and Adult Inquirers Classes/New Member Courses. I have enjoyed sharing much of what is found in this text in private one-on-one conversations with inquirers in my study. Sometimes I have been able to provide insights about Presbyterians over the telephone with questioning Presbyterians from over the nation, including disheartened ministers and angry church officers. Always I seek both to be truthful (realistic) and hopeful (optimistic), in the proper balance.

I am grateful to those who took the time to critique the first drafts of this book and to offer suggestions for improvement and encouragement: Mary Bishop, Charles Schechner, and Robert H. Thompson of Highland Park; Albert L. Gillin of Lubbock, Texas, and James B. Harper of San Antonio, Texas, my former seminary interns; and Roger A. Kvam, Greer, South Carolina, and Nancy Maffett, Colorado Springs, Colorado, from the leadership of Presbyterians for Renewal. The session of Highland Park Church and senior minister, B. Clayton Bell Sr., offered study leave in which this project could be completed. Jean Jenney, my administrative assistant, warm friend, and ally in new member ministry, protected my time, fulfilled all needed work details, and encouraged me along the way by covering other work obligations by which I was freed for this writing. I am much obliged to my colleague of many years, Pat McGeachy, Nolensville, Tennessee, for his insightful illustrations, which brighten and lighten an otherwise "heavy" approach to a delightful subject.

The goodness of God is often most clearly seen in those whom He places closest to us in our long journey of Christian service. No one could be more blessed by a supportive family and colleagues than I. I am thankful to God. May this text be used winsomely to win persons to Jesus Christ and to membership in local Presbyterian churches and to encourage the Presbyterian flock in our pilgrimage through time and space to obedience and faithfulness to our sovereign God.

PRESBYTERIANS: PEOPLE OF THE MIDDLE WAY

Welcome!

You have been invited either because you have expressed an interest in becoming a member of this Presbyterian church or because you are curious and want to find out about Christianity and Presbyterians!

We shall seek the answers to the following questions:

From a Presbyterian viewpoint what makes one a Christian?

How does one become a Presbyterian?

Where did Presbyterian Christians come from?

What is unique about Presbyterian Christians?

How do Presbyterian Christians differ from other Christians?

What generally do Presbyterian Christians believe?

How do Presbyterian Christians govern themselves?

Can one help me understand Presbyterian worship and mission?

What is the history, character, and expectations of this local congregation?

Should I decide to join, what are the benefits and how may I serve?

Tell me again how to join!

Opening Prayer and Introductions

A lay host calls the meeting to order, leads in the opening prayer, and introduces other lay hosts, any deacons, or other current members who are a part of the leadership team, as he/she welcomes all the prospects and inquirers to the meeting. This host then turns the meeting over to the teacher in charge.

Get Acquainted—Small Group Discussions

I join in welcoming you here today. God has some wonderful surprises and blessings in store for each of us, as we learn more about Him and His expectations, as we learn more about the Presbyterian Church and about this local congregation in which you have interest, and as we make new friends and gain new spiritual insights.

Momentarily we will be dividing into small discussion groups of five or six prospects/inquirers with one host. Because time is limited and we want everyone to have a chance to participate, we have asked the host to get you started and stopped on time and to encourage you to move quickly around your circle as you discuss the following questions:

1. Share about yourself and your family (where applicable): name, spouse, children, where you are from, your work, what brought you to our area, and any other important background information.

2. Describe your previous church background, if any.

3. What attracted you to this local Presbyterian church?

Now please move into circles of about six or seven persons, including one host per group. Your host will help you use our fifteen minutes of small group time wisely.

Course Overview, Schedule, and Expectations

Now that we are back in plenary session we are ready to take an overview of the course of study before us.

Please turn to page 1 of our *Student Text* and browse with me as we review the eleven questions we intend to answer during this class series. As you can tell, we expect to deal with such subjects as: "What makes one a Christian?" "How one becomes a Presbyterian and why?" "Presbyterian origins and history, uniqueness, ethos, and personality," "Presbyterian beliefs, governance, worship, and mission," "Data about this local congregation, its history, character, ministry, mission, and your future part in it (should you so chose)," as well as "How you may plug in immediately and effectively into both the benefits of church membership and the privileges of service through your new congregation." We assume you are here because you wish to know the answers to these questions and have either a commitment to moving forward towards membership or a curiosity to discover "just who these Presbyterians are."

Now turn with me to pages vii–viii of the *Student Text*. Here you will see how we plan in a six-hour time frame to provide these answers and to introduce you to several current church members so that you may hear what they have to say either about their membership or about a particular aspect of our church ministry. You will also note that we plan to have a good time with much group interaction where you can make new friends.

Please check the schedule posted on the board to note the days, times, and places for each of our six lessons.

You should expect us to make these hours informative and reasonably entertaining. We hope when we finish you will be able to join numbers of others who declare that this experience was very worthwhile and enjoyable.

In turn, we ask you to attempt to attend the entire class schedule, arriving early enough to enable us to start on time. We ask you to read what portions of the *Student Text* you can and browse the rest. (This text will also serve you as a reference book which you may wish to retain in your library for further reflection on Presbyterianism.) We ask you to be open and honest with us about your continuing questions and doubts. We ask you to make your own decision and not be influenced by the "herd instinct." We do not want you to join this local church if you are not ready or convinced that this is God's special place for you at this time.

Announcements and Explanations

Most of you are "prospects," which means that between you and me we have agreed that you have significant interest in the possibility of becoming a member of this church, either because of your involvement in our congregation's life, or because of your family connections or your scheduled wedding, or because of your interest in what you think we have to offer, or because in some way God has led you to the door of our family. We welcome you, though we still expect you to use your God-given judgment as to whether in the final analysis you wish to pursue membership. By the end of the fourth lesson we should like to know your intention regarding completing the membership process.

Others of you are "inquirers," persons with sincere curiosity who want to know "just who we Presbyterian Christians are." This curiosity may arise out of your own faith-commitments to other world religions or to other Christian denominations, or perhaps out of your interest in the belief-system of your spouse or your fiancé. In any case, you have marked your class application card with a capital "I," denoting your attendance as an inquirer. Therefore, neither you nor I will expect any follow-up action on your part or any membership completion. You are like an auditor in an academic setting with no obligations, though, of course, at the end of the class you have the freedom to choose to join this church.

[Note: The suggestions below are appropriate for the classes I teach, but each teacher in each particular church will have special needs and unique arrangements to announce to the class. Please adjust as needed.]

All of us have nametags. Leaders and helpers in teaching this course have blue nametags. All students have white nametags. The dot system tells us from a distance more about you: a blue dot tells us we already have your class application card; a red dot tells us we

already have your photograph; and an orange dot tells us that you are already a member of this local congregation and are taking a refresher course, perhaps with a spouse or fiancé. You are all welcome!

Directions for finding the rest rooms are listed on the board. (When we have a four-hour session there will be one formal break about mid-morning, but you are encouraged to take your own additional breaks, as needed, by quietly slipping out of your chair and finding the rest rooms or the refreshments which are visible to us all.)

(When the course is taught as a one-weekend series, the church may provide a complimentary new member luncheon at the conclusion of the Saturday session. Following such a lunch it may be a good idea to provide the class the option of a short tour of the church facility for those interested and able to stay.)

How To Become a Christian
From a Presbyterian Viewpoint

[Note: Each teacher should speak here from his/her own experience.] Over the time I have been teaching these classes approximately 10 percent of those who have become members of this church have made "adult professions of faith"; that means they had not heretofore joined any church or ever been confirmed. They had never before publicly declared themselves to be Christians, on the side of Christ.

With this fact etched upon my mind I do not hesitate to ask the rest of you, those who are already members of some church, to listen to this elementary, though essential, discussion of how one becomes a Christian. Who knows, even we who have long belonged to Jesus Christ might yet learn something which may prove helpful.

What Is a Christian?

A Christian is one who is saved from sin by the initiative of God in His grace through faith in Him, a faith He places in our hearts which allows us to respond to Him in love, holiness, and obedience.

A Christian is a follower of Jesus Christ, one who learns from Him, seeks to love and obey Him, attempts to live the moral life Christ would have us live, and seeks to serve Him by serving others.

A Christian is a believer in Jesus Christ, who acknowledges Him as both the Son of God and one's own sufficient personal Savior from sin.

A Christian is a lover of the triune God through Jesus Christ, one who seeks to reflect God's love in all relationships with others.

A Christian is one who by God's grace attempts to think Christ's thoughts after Him, to do Christ's deeds for others; in other

words, one who seeks to be Christ's hands and feet in a lost and hurting world.

Relationship, Not Deeds

In understanding what makes one a Christian, it is critically important to know that it is the relationship which counts for everything; it is the means by which we "are born again or anew" into a son/daughter relationship with God the Father through the power of the Holy Spirit (Who is God present with us today).

> In reply Jesus declared, "I tell you the truth, no one can see the kingdom of God unless he is born again. . . . For God so loved the world that he gave his one and only Son, that whoever believes in him shall not perish but have eternal life." (John 3:3, 16)

God's salvation is not earned by our merits, good deeds, wonderful behavior, attendance at church, personal morality, public service, or anything of human origin. These all are important fruit of the new creation in Christ birthed by God's initiative and valid only as relationship.

> Therefore, if anyone is in Christ, he is a new creation; the old has gone, the new has come! All this is from God, who reconciled us to himself through Christ and gave us the ministry of reconciliation:

that God was reconciling the world to himself in Christ, not counting men's sins against them. (2 Corinthians 5:17–19a)

Indeed, it can be truly said that genuine Christianity is really "a personal relationship with God," not a formalized religion of rules and requirements, though those "rightly related to God" do eventually reflect the character of God in our deeds.

> To some who were confident of their own righteousness and looked down on everybody else, Jesus told this parable: "Two men went up to the temple to pray, one a Pharisee and the other a tax collector. The Pharisee stood up and prayed about himself: 'God, I thank you that I am not like other men—robbers, evildoers, adulterers—or even like this tax collector. I fast twice a week and give a tenth of all I get.'
>
> "But the tax collector stood at a distance. He would not even look up to heaven, but beat his breast and said, 'God, have mercy on me, a sinner.' I tell you that this man, rather than the other, went home justified before God." (Luke 18:9–14a)

To say the same thing differently, a Christian is *not* defined by:

church membership	pristine morality
being philanthropic or generous	helping people
being pro-life or pro-choice	being "religious"
being pro-environment or anti-war	sterling character
being a change agent in the political arena	public service
becoming a martyr for good causes	living a godly life
supporting charity	good deeds

Many have given the wrong answer when asked: "If you were to die tonight and be carried to the gate of heaven and were asked why you should be let into God's heaven, what would be your best answer?" (This question in somewhat the same form was first framed by D. James Kennedy in his "Evangelism Explosion" program.)

"My church membership" won't give you a place.

"Look at my lifetime of helping the poor" is unacceptable.

"I've been a faithful spouse, a good parent, and obedient child" will not pass. Good works and fine character simply will not pass muster at the entry into heaven.

The only acceptable answer for an eternity with God in heaven is "I trusted in Jesus Christ and His death on the Cross for me and my sins; I believe in Him."

Sin Separates the Human Race from God

This is the universal problem we all face, but God has provided the only acceptable answer in the Cross of Christ.

> Jesus answered, "I am the way and the truth and the life. No one comes to the Father except through me." (John 14:6)

God's Grace in Christ Reestablishes the Broken Relationship

Christianity deals with human sin and how to get rid of it. Only those who admit that they share in the problem of all humanity are eligible for God's redemptive love in Jesus Christ. Sin is the problem; God's grace in Christ is the answer.

> I am not ashamed of the gospel, because it is the power of God for the salvation of everyone who believes: first for the Jew, then for the Gentile. . . . There is no difference, for all have sinned and fall short of the glory of God, and are justified freely by his grace through the redemption that came by Christ Jesus. God presented him as a sacrifice of atonement, through faith in his blood. . . . Therefore, there is now no condemnation for those who are in Christ Jesus. . . . (Romans 1:16; 3:22b–25a; 8:1)

Another Good Way of Answering the Question

"How does one become a Christian" can be answered by thoroughly understanding and committing to three action words: Repent—Believe—Accept. These words are explained on the following several pages and are basic to our entire course of study.

Repent

If our human dilemma is sin, we need to be sure we understand what sin is. A modern definition of sin is "anything which we think, believe, or do that is less than God's best intention for us." Thus, sin can be right things left unthought or undone; sin can be bad things thought or done. Sin is our mismatch with God's perfect expectation for His human children. Sin can involve attitude as well as action, heart as well as hand.

The first step towards becoming a Christian is to face the fact that each one of us is a sinner in the eyes of God, needing His redemption, correction, and salvation. God has taken the initiative through His love (which, when undeserved, we call grace) in sending His Son Jesus Christ to take upon Himself all the penalty due us for our sin.

For the broken relationship between God and humankind to be reknit, God has taken the first step. Our first step is admitting that we have erred, sinned, failed, fallen short of His expectation or glory.

Such an admission requires repentance. To repent in Greek means "to change one's mind" or "to alter one's direction" or "to turn around and go another way."

> As the sergeant screamed his order to his company of men marching east, "About face, march!" they turned as one and began marching west.
>
> Saul of Tarsus thought he was honoring God by participating in the death of Christians until Jesus confronted him on the road to Damascus. Saul repented of his actions, altered his behavior, became a Christian himself, and sought to spread the Gospel to all the known Roman world as "Paul the Apostle." His life direction was totally changed, reversed, corrected, as he sought to obey God. This change of direction is the biblical meaning of repent. (see Acts 9:1–30)

Believe

Repenting of our sin is the first step in entering into right relationship with God. But in a sense, repentance is a negative; it is doing something about the obstacle between God and us.

The second essential step in becoming a Christian is a positive, believing that God has already provided the bridge between humankind and God in the Cross of Jesus Christ! We are called to believe in Jesus Christ as our personal Savior and Lord.

There is something weak in our usage of the English word *believe*, while the Greek word translated *believe* is always much stronger. In English *believe* may indicate simply "an inclination to agree," "to acknowledge that something may be true." It sometimes is a "cheap word." Not so in Greek, for in Greek the verb *believe* always takes a different preposition than we use in English. In English we say "I believe in"; in Greek the language says "I believe into." There is commitment; indeed, often a commitment of life! May I illustrate by an old story I have often heard.

> Back in the days somewhere between Buffalo Bill and Batman, back in the days before television, the public's craving for adventure often took the form of admiration of daredevils such as Blondin, a world-famous tightrope artist, who at the height of his career, we are told, made it safely over a cable stretched above Niagara Falls from Canada to America before a crowd of several hundred thousand raving admirers.  Not only was he able to walk safely across several times, but he pushed a specially built wheelbarrow from one country to the other without incident. Then, to cap off his spectacular feat he placed his trusty sidekick Joe into the wheelbarrow and pushed him safely across, to the stifling roar and approval of the masses. When he had finished, and Joe safely descended from the cable tower, Blondin spotted an excited boy of eleven in the crowd. "Billy," he called out, "do you believe I can take you safely across in my wheelbarrow?" "You bet, Mr. Blondin," exclaimed a confident Billy. "Okay then," challenged Blondin, "Get in!" Billy got lost in the crowd!

Billy believed in Mr. Blondin with an English "believe in," while Joe believed in Mr. Blondin with a Greek "believe into"! The difference was commitment of life! Will you believe into Jesus Christ and bet your life on Him? This is the second step.

Accept

> **Step 1:** Repent of my sins; that is, "truly to turn around and go another way."

> **Step 2:** Believe "into" Jesus Christ (with a costly commitment of life).

> **Step 3:** Personally appropriate Him as my own personal Savior and Lord and not just the theoretical Savior and Lord of "the world" or of "somebody else."

A dying illiterate derelict was brought into a rescue mission from the gutter, a prodigal loved by someone, though they knew not who. The chaplain and the nurse did the best they could for his comfort of both body and soul. As the chaplain read to him John 3:16 ("For God so loved the world that he gave his one and only Son, that whoever believes in him shall not perish but have eternal life."), the dying man in one of his last gasps of life whispered: "Sign my name to dat verse" and died.

He understood the truth that for God's salvation to work and be applied personally for him he must "sign my name to dat verse!"

> I have a beautifully wrapped present here for one of you. [I randomly select a recipient.] Marie, this is for you. I am bringing it to you; it is a gift to you from me. It is yours if you will perfectly illustrate how a gracious one receives a genuine gift. What three things will you do for this gift to be yours? Right, you first open your hands and appropriate it and take it to yourself. Then, second, you correctly have just verbally thanked me. Now third, you most likely will open it in my presence and again thank me as you claim it for yourself. Yes, the gift is really yours to keep!

Marie, you have just illustrated the three things I as a human being must do to "appropriate" God's gift for me of eternal life in Jesus Christ. I must: (1) take it, appropriate it, "accept" it, as really meant for me; (2) thank God for it; and (3) open the gift and put my personal acceptance mark on it.

Is this not what accept means in this context of God's love for me?

> Yet to all who received him, to those who believed in his name, he gave the right to become children of God. (John 1:12)

This is not the only way to describe the magnificent experience of becoming a Christian, but it is an effective one, one which works, one which honors God's revealed truth and which gently allows the individual freedom to chose to belong to the heavenly Father.

Have you already "repented, believed into, and accepted" God's way of salvation? Are you now ready, perhaps for the first time, to "repent, believe into, and accept" God at His word? If so, then you may want to join with me in offering the following prayer, which some of us have often made, but for others today this may be your first time.

Some may wish to sign and date this prayer in the quiet of your home tonight, as a very important date and event in your eternal life.

> And this is the testimony: God has given us eternal life, and this life is in his Son. He who has the Son has life; he who does not have the Son of God does not have life. I write these things to you who believe in the name of the Son of God so that you may know that you have eternal life. (1 John 5:11–13)

If you have sincerely asked Jesus to come into your heart, He has. Now your task is to believe it, whether you feel it or not. Believe it! Act on it! You are now His!

Dear heavenly Father, thank You for creating me and placing me in Your world. Thank You for the capacity of having fellowship with You. I am sorry that my sin has come between us; I do now, as much as I know how, repent of my sin and promise, as much as I know how, to allow You to change me and my habits and my way of life, so that I may be more pleasing to You. Please forgive me for living separately from You. I do now, as much as I know how, believe into Jesus Christ as the Son of God and my personal Savior. I do now, as much as I know how, accept You personally and invite You into my life to clean me up, to redirect me, and to control me with Your Spirit of love. Please give me a place to grow spiritually in the fellowship of Your Church. Please make me a new creation so that I may enjoy, through being born again, Your new and eternal world, both now and always. I love You; I trust You; I want to follow You. Please empower me. Thank You, God. I pray in Jesus' name. Amen.

Date:_____

Name:_____

Let Us Now Summarize What We Have Learned
- A Christian is one who is saved from our own sin
    is a believer into Jesus Christ
    is a lover of God and His Son Jesus Christ
    is a follower of Jesus Christ
    is one who by God's grace attempts to think Christ's
        thoughts after Him

- God's salvation is not earned; it is a free gift.

- Genuine Christianity is really "a personal relationship with God."

- A Christian is not defined by deeds but by a relationship with God in Christ.

- Sin has separated the human race from God; but God's grace in Christ reestablishes this broken relationship.

- A true, yet simple, way of understanding how I may become a Christian is:

    1. To repent of my sins

    2. To believe "into" Jesus Christ as Savior

    3. To accept Him personally as my Lord

- God answers the prayer of the heart, believing "as much as I know how." The one, who, in faith, prays a prayer of confession and belief and acceptance, is His!

> If we confess our sins, he is faithful and just and will forgive us our sins and purify us from all unrighteousness. (1 John 1:9)

> For there is no difference between Jew and Gentile—the same Lord is Lord of all and richly blesses all who call on him, for, "Everyone who calls on the name of the Lord will be saved." (Romans 10:12–13)

> "Salvation is found in no one else, for there is no other name under heaven given to men by which we must be saved." (Acts 4:12)

• When one enters into faith,

> the believer needs to make this new faith public as quickly as is
> comfortable
>
> the believer seeks to make God the controlling factor in life
>
> the believer will have a different way to invest in life and in
> leisure
>
> the believer will find a new heart for sharing generously with
> those in need
>
> the believer will discover a new attitude towards the poor and
> those less fortunate
>
> the believer soon will find
>> a new value system
>> a new want system
>> a new world view
>> a new way of life
>> a new way of treating others
>> a new way of doing business
>> a new way of relating to family, neighbors, and enemies

The Church will be the believer's new family. Together they will
be fellow strugglers, fellow witnesses, fellow pilgrims, and Jesus' own
hands and feet.

Now What Does a Christian Do?

> We thirst for a knowledge of God's Word.
>
> We discover the joy of conversation (prayer) with our heavenly Father.
>
> We find that we can tell others about our new spiritual life with less embarrassment.
>
> We discover a deep desire for regular worship and fellowship with God.
>
> We now want to help others come to a saving knowledge of God in Christ.
>
> We urgently desire the fellowship of other Christians and find how important is a regular relationship with the Church as a family of faith.
>
> We seek to fulfill God's plan for our life.
>
> We seek good places to invest cheerfully and generously God's portion of our income.

How To Become a Presbyterian

The requirements for membership in any local Presbyterian Church include (1) a personal faith in Jesus Christ as Savior and Lord and (2) a willingness to be subject to the leadership of the church.

Local procedures may differ. In all cases the session is obligated to question the membership candidate to discover his/her personal faith in Jesus Christ. [Note: At the time of reunion (1983) two sets of membership questions were recommended. Some sessions use the following questions:

> (Name), who is your Lord and Savior? Do you trust in Him? Do you intend to be His disciple, to obey His word and to show His love? Will you be a faithful member of this congregation, giving of yourself in every way, and will you seek the fellowship of the Church wherever you may be?

However, the primary set of questions (church vows) found on the next page has long been the approved questions for my session.]

The following procedure for joining this particular local church is highly recommended. [Note: Teachers should feel free to adapt this course of study to the church vows approved by their session. Where no one set has been approved, I recommend adoption of those found on page 19. I have found the following Three Step procedure plus Service of Recognition most helpful. Rule of thumb: adapt where necessary; follow where appropriate.]

> **Step 1:** Candidates meet with a group of church officers to discuss their interest in membership and to fill out application cards which begin the process.

Step 2: Candidates are expected to attend a six-hour Adult Inquirers Class/New Member Course series, where they learn about the Presbyterian Church, the meaning of membership, and the various opportunities for service and growth at this local church.

Step 3: Candidates meet with the session at the conclusion of the Adult Inquirers Class/New Member Course, where each new member candidate is introduced and asked to affirm or reaffirm the five Church Vows of membership in the PC(USA).

Service of Recognition: New members will then receive certificates of membership and letters of invitation to a "recognition service," which is held in the sanctuary periodically, as needed. This is followed by a reception in honor of these most recent new members. If one is uniting with the church by profession of faith and baptism, then at that worship service baptism is offered, as this completes the membership process for him/her.

The Five Church Vows for membership in my particular local church are as follows and become the outline for this chapter on "How To Become a Presbyterian."

FIVE CHURCH VOWS

1.   Do you acknowledge yourself to be a sinner
     in the sight of God,
     justly deserving God's displeasure
     and without hope
     except in God's sovereign mercy?

                                                    Answer: I do!

2.   Do you believe in the Lord Jesus Christ
     as the Son of God
     and Savior of sinners,
     and do you receive and depend upon Christ alone
     for your salvation
     as offered in the Gospel?

                                                    Answer: I do!

3.   Do you now resolve and promise,
     in humble reliance upon the grace
     of the Holy Spirit, that you will endeavor
     to live as becomes the followers of Christ?

                                                    Answer: I do!

4.   Do you promise to serve Christ
     in the Church
     by supporting and participating
     in its service to God
     and its ministry to others
     to the best of your ability?

                                                    Answer: I do!

5.   Do you submit yourself
     to the government
     and discipline
     of the Church
     and promise to further
     its purity and peace?

                                                    Answer: I do!

The above questions were a part of the PCUS constitution for many years and were
continued by the reuniting PC(USA) until a revision of the "Directory for Worship" in
1988. By action of this local church session all new members must affirm or reaffirm
these Five Church Vows.

Basic Statements about the Presbyterian Church

The head of the Presbyterian Church is not the General Assembly nor the assembly moderator or stated clerk nor the presbytery nor the session nor the minister nor any of the many helpful "Confessions (Statements) of Faith" which Presbyterians use. No, the only head of the Presbyterian Church is Jesus Christ Himself!

Presbyterians state quite strongly that "God alone is Lord of the·· conscience."

Presbyterians believe that God created human beings with minds as well as hearts and therefore expects Presbyterian members to become educated and informed about all of life, including matters of faith and practice. It should not surprise anyone that Presbyterians do not look to their leadership to tell them what is right and wrong, but all members are responsible for the study of God's Word and the discovery of God's revealed will for themselves.

Presbyterians, as thinking people, differ on occasion and do not always look at things exactly alike. In fact, among Presbyterians there are many differences, yet there is a commitment to a unifying faith core (essential tenets of the Reformed Faith) which holds Presbyterians together.

Presbyterians strongly believe we are but part of the Church of the Lord Jesus Christ; therefore we recognize God at work in the ecumenical Church, which includes most of the denominations from which you in this class have come. In practice this means that we joyfully accept what God has already done in your life in your former congregations and denominations. We do not rebaptize any who have been baptized elsewhere with water and in the Name of the Holy · Trinity. We accept your Christian experiences in most other churches, though there are a few exceptions (primarily those groups which are cultic in nature.)

To be a member of the Presbyterian Church one must affirm but five questions (those we have read and are about to explain), and only five. However, we do hold to a kind of healthy double standard, in that we seek to include any Christian anywhere as a member of our church family of faith if that be their wish, but we carefully require all our officers (including ministers, elders, and deacons) to "receive and adopt the essential tenets of the Reformed faith as expressed in the confessions of our church as authentic and reliable expositions of what Scripture leads us to believe and do. . . ." (*Book of Order*,

G-14.0405b(3)) What this means for you is that you, as members, are responsible for but five questions, while we who are church officers must affirm what amounts to ten thousand questions about the Reformed Faith.

Among Protestants (that is, heirs of the sixteenth century Reformation in Europe) Presbyterians are basically "middle people" with whom most other Protestants can at least partially feel comfortable.

The Meaning of These Five Church Vows

Question 1: Sin

Do you acknowledge yourself to be a sinner in the sight of God, justly deserving God's displeasure and without hope except in God's sovereign mercy?

The Presbyterian Church is only open for sinners, failures, and the helpless. Perfect people and sinless people need not apply. The more discerning and mature a Christian is, in our view, the more he/she sees his/her own sin, as God sees it. The mature Presbyterian Christian prays regularly: "Lord, forgive my sins of this day in thought, word, and deed."

> In the year that King Uzziah died, I saw the Lord seated on a throne, high and exalted, and the train of his robe filled the temple. Above him were seraphs, each with six wings. . . . And they were calling to one another: "Holy, holy, holy is the Lord Almighty; the whole earth is full of his glory." At the sound of their voices the doorposts and thresholds shook and the temple was filled with smoke. "Woe to me!" I cried. "I am ruined! For I am a man of unclean lips, and I live among a people of unclean lips, and my eyes have seen the King, the Lord Almighty." Then one of the seraphs flew to me with a live coal in his hand, which he had taken with tongs from the altar. With it he touched my mouth and said, "See, this has touched your lips; your guilt is taken away and your sin atoned for." (Isaiah 6:1–7)

We do see sin in our own lives; we do see sin everywhere. Our first parents rebelled against God in the Garden; since then, all of us have lived out our propensity to sin. In a sense Adam and Eve were "Everyman/Everywoman" of the medieval morality plays. They could not handle the innocence and choice with which they were created; they, like all their children, rebelled against God. This sin is the problem the Presbyterian Church seeks to answer by acknowledging that we have just such a problem.

I am reminded of what transpired in our earliest pastorate in Concord, Tennessee, as my wife and I were seeking to provide a safe environment for our two-year-old son. We lived in the manse a half-block from the main highway between Knoxville and Chattanooga. To the far side of the highway lay the main rail line between those two larger cities. Then on the far side of the railway was a large lake. Hence, there were three death-traps for a rambling two year old whose parents could not then provide an enclosed fence about the backyard for a safe play area. What does one do when safety is a factor in showing love for a inquisitive and roaming young son?

We decided to build an internal fence within the conscience of our son by clearly marking in his mind the "edge of our safe property" in which he was free to roam and play; outside this boundary was a clear, unmistaken "no" with severe warnings of punishment if necessary. He and I walked with his little hand wrapped tightly about my finger around the edge of the property, clearly saying "inside, yes," "outside, no." We did this over and over again until we were convinced he understood "the rules of love." For weeks we sought to reinforce this training.

At last we believed he was ready for the test of obedience for his own life's sake. He was permitted to go outside, down the steep back steps into the backyard, equipped with pleasant reminders of the "yes-ness" of inside and the "no-ness"of "beyond our property." Mother and Daddy stayed inside to observe our trainee. Quickly and happily he ran to every corner of the approved "inside" of the backyard; then he spotted Miss Mattie's house next door, across the boundary line. Apparently inside his heart he decided that he desired to roam to Miss Mattie's more than he wished to obey his parents. We saw him run to the farthest corner of the "inside" approved property, lift his foot high off the ground as though stepping over a little fence marker, and then leaping to place both feet onto the "forbidden off-limits" he skipped to the attractive neighbor's home, to which he bolted in glee, not without two parents leaping down the back steps, each grabbing an offending hand of a disobedient son. We soon got to "the bottom of this disobedience problem." A repetition of this several times brought us to the place where we had a trained and obedient son whom we could trust. In the process of such rules, totally constructed on love for his life, Hal grew in safety to manhood; sadly, we could not teach our dog, Smokey Joe, these same lessons; we lost this disobedient dog to a car on the highway that year. Here is another illustration of the misuse of freedom, the story of Adam and Eve all over again; it is the story of "Everyman."

We acknowledge that God is holy and we are unholy and therefore stand condemned in God's eyes, unless there is mercy. We see ourselves unable to save ourselves; we are "without hope, except in God's sovereign mercy." Presbyterians speak often of the sovereignty of God, which means God "is in control," "has a plan," "is omnipotent enough to accomplish His purpose," and "is the eternal and for-always Number One of the Universe!"

Question 2: Salvation

Do you believe in the Lord Jesus Christ as the Son of God and Savior of sinners, and do you receive and depend upon Christ alone for your salvation as offered in the gospel?

If question one described the human problem of sin, then question two quickly gets to God's solution: His salvation freely offered in Jesus Christ, His Son, Who by dying on the Cross, provided eternal salvation from sin to all who willingly accept Him. (Here we are reminded of the suggested formula for becoming a Christian: repent, believe (into), and accept.) Indeed, it is fair to say that from a

Presbyterian viewpoint these first two questions, expected of new members, exactly describe our Presbyterian understanding of sin and salvation, of our human dilemma and God's solution. Therefore, from our perspective, anyone who is genuinely a Christian should be able joyfully to affirm these questions one and two!

You should note that Presbyterians understand that God's salvation is found in Jesus alone, not in Jesus and the Church, Jesus and the sacraments, Jesus and good works, Jesus and high morality. God's salvation is found in Jesus alone. This salvation is offered in the gospel; that is, found in the Bible, which is the place where we human beings can discover the gospel.

One other thing needs to be said about the Presbyterian perspective. We fully admit we do not gloss over human sin; we call it as we see it: sin is rebellion against God. Yet, for all the emphasis Presbyterians put on sin, we seek overwhelmingly to place greater emphasis on and call more attention to God's grace, which is His love we don't deserve. "But where sin increased, grace increased all the more . . ." (Romans 5:20b).

Presbyterians, of all Christians, seem ready to name sin for what it is, but we also of all Christians are even more ready to broadcast the sunburst of God's grace, a grace which covers all confessed sin and which redeems to the uttermost!

> In the fable of the Sun and the Cave, we hear the two bragging about their respective powers, perhaps at the annual convention of fable characters. Mr. Cave eloquently describes the total darkness within his deepest caverns, so dark that nothing can ever be seen. Dr. Sun explains that he has never seen darkness, only brightness all his days. Mr. Cave then invites Dr. Sun to visit him "one day soon." Sometime later Dr. Sun knocks on the door of Mr. Cave's residence and is invited in for a tour of these darkest regions. But everywhere Dr. Sun moves within the precincts of Mr. Cave, there is no darkness at all, only the brightest light ever seen. Wherever Dr. Sun goes, there is light and no darkness at all!

Presbyterians ever are learning that God's grace is like the sun, and human sin is like the cave darkness: wherever the grace of God is found, human sin in its darkness fades, is overwhelmed by God's forgiveness, and is covered by the grace and light of God. That is how much God's grace overwhelms and covers our human sin.

"Then neither do I condemn you," Jesus declared. "Go now and leave your life of sin." (John 8:11b)

"Therefore, there is now no condemnation for those who are in Christ Jesus. . . ." (Romans 8:1)

Question 3: Sanctification

Do you now resolve and promise, in humble reliance upon the grace of the Holy Spirit, that you will endeavor to live as becomes the followers of Christ?

There are three parts to this question; each is extremely important for the seeker to understand: there is the effort to be made, the goal to be reached, and the promised Helper along the way.

First, we are making a solemn promise before God and the public that we shall indeed make every effort possible; that is, "to endeavor" to become something we have not yet attained. We recognize that the Christian life is a journey, the destination of which is still unreached.

We understand that progress has both its forward gear and its reverse gear, that sometimes we turn to the left or to the right. Maturity is not without its bumps, its slips, its slides, its backward movements, but we promise to hang on for the whole journey.

Second, the goal to be reached is a life that is consistent with God's intention for us human beings; that is, "a life which becomes the followers of Christ." This is biblical talk for a decent, moral, uplifting, God-honoring life of holy and joyful living as children of the heavenly Father. Presbyterians are not perfectionists, for we know that no human being can live the perfect life here on earth. The best a Presbyterian can ever hope for is to become Ivory soap Christians, which are (if you remember the ancient radio commercial) "99 and 44/100ths percent pure." That's the max for Presbyterians! But, this is our goal! For Presbyterians moral perfection can only be finally attained in heaven: ". . . he who began a good work in you will carry it on to completion until the day of Christ Jesus" (Philippians 1:6b).

Third, Presbyterians know that the journey, hard as it may be, is not traveled alone, for God promises His Comforter, His Holy Spirit, "God-present-today," to walk beside us and at times to carry us. I know I certainly cannot make it through my life without this Divine Helper every day. I am also glad God gives us one another as fellow encouragers and pioneers along the way to the Celestial City.

Once upon a time, so the story goes, there was in dry and rough West Texas a ranch with a dusty road which ran between the barn and the house. There it seldom rained, but when it did, that road turned into a series of mud puddles. After a rare rain, out pranced a lamb followed by a roaming piglet, as they moved down the road towards the house. The pig leaped from mudhole to mudhole soaking up the dirty puddles and making ripples in the water with his curly tail; he was obviously dirty and getting dirtier, for "playing in mudholes" is in the nature of a piglet! However, the pampered lamb sought diligently to avoid every mudhole and any speck of mud, unsuccessfully on that day, of course. It was in the nature of the lamb to seek to avoid the mudholes and keep his wool as clean as possible.

The human being without Jesus Christ has a nature which allows him to "enjoy the mud and filth of this world," while the person who trusts in Jesus Christ and has a new nature seeks to avoid the mudholes

and sins of this world in order to grow more like the Master. Friends, we who are in Christ must ever remember that we have been given the nature of the Lamb, and no longer have we the nature of the pig! Let us endeavor to live like the lamb and avoid the way of the pig.

Question 4: Service

Do you promise to serve Christ in the Church by supporting and participating in its service to God and its ministry to others to the best of your ability?

There are four parts to this vow. First, we are making a promise to Jesus Christ; second, the locus for our promise-keeping is within the church; third, the nature of our promise is two-fold: worship and work; and lastly, we make this promise measuring our progress not by the abilities of any others, but by "our own best ability."

We should always remember our promises are made to please God and His Son, not to please the preacher or the church family or even our own family. We are not taking up challenges to meet our personal ego needs; we are instead making a solemn vow to none other than the One who hung on the tree for me! Thus, such a promise is very personal. We even take as our primary new name the name of Christ in "Christian."

> Alexander the Great was within an inch of conquering the known world, when he rode upon a court marital within his ranks. Stopping his steed, he called to the captain for an explanation. Said the officer of the young recruit about to be beheaded for desertion, "Sir, this scoundrel deserted us in a moment of blazing battle, and I am about to give him his just deserves." Alexander for a moment had pity in his heart and cried out to the deserter: "Boy, what is your name?" "Alexander, sir, I'm sorry," he wept. In rage Alexander the Great, infuriated that one with his name would ever desert, granted clemency and roared: "Boy, change your behavior or change your name!"

I can hear Jesus Christ order each of us: "Change your behavior or change your name!"

If we seek to worship God and serve humankind, there are many ways these good works can be done. But I have found, with millions of others through the centuries, that God's gift of the Church, as a group of fellow seekers and servants living within a family of faith, makes it easier for me to be a Christian and to practice my Christianity. Being social creatures, we tend to do many things better when we are partnered with others. I suspect our Bible study and our care for the poor can be done more effectively if we become part of a team. John Calvin was so convinced of the value of the gathered saints of God as church that he may have exaggerated the truth when he declared: "As God is our Father, so the Church is our mother." But I am thankful that the place where most of my worship and service can be done is in my local parish church with others like you. Won't you too become habituated to such a life of partnership with other Christians within your chosen family of faith?

When we promise to "support and participate in the Church's service to God," I interpret this to mean that I plan to be present as an active worshiper every time I can make it. I plan to do my part; I plan to find my part. I will use my gifts where best needed. I will support my church with my regular presence, my willing involvement, my generous financial underwriting, and my cheerful and agreeable spirit, both in worship to God and ministry to others. This means that I will find at least one place where I can make a difference through my church in the lives of others.

Lastly, I thank God that I am not vowing "to keep up with the Jones'" nor anyone else. I am grateful that we are not measured in church by equal expectations of everyone, whether it be teaching skills, attendance habits, financial contributions, or time spent in specific ministries. I understand that God and I are the "measurers," and we measure me "by my own best ability," given all my circumstances and situations.

> "Then the righteous will answer him, 'Lord, when did we see you hungry and feed you, or thirsty and give you something to drink? When did we see you a stranger and invite you in, or needing clothes and clothe you? When did we see you sick or in prison and go to visit you?' The King will reply, 'I tell you the truth, whatever you did for one of the least of these brothers of mine, you did for me.'" (Matthew 25:37–40)

Question 5: Submission

Do you submit yourself to the government and discipline of the Church and promise to further its purity and peace?

Presbyterians, as we shall see later, do not live under an autocratic government, nor are we a pure democracy where "all the people all the time have all the say"; instead, we have a republican, representative form of government, much like the United States government at its best "of the people, by the people, and for the people." In our system all members have a voice and vote in selecting their ministers and their elders. The elders, then, as our representatives meet to make the decisions for the spiritual good of the congregation. Thus, when we declare before God and the session that we freely submit ourselves "to the government . . . of the Church," we are submitting to ourselves. Presbyterianism is a form of partnership where we work together for the common good.

For those who seriously misbehave there is a Rules of Discipline book by which we correct ourselves, again always for the honor of the name of Christ and for the common good.

Please note that the word "Church" is capitalized both in question four and question five. This capitalization means that we are committing not only to "the local congregation" but also "to the national denomination." In our case, that means the Presbyterian Church (U.S.A.), the main body of American Presbyterians, numbering about 2.8 million of us, with a history which goes back in this country to 1706 and whose continental roots go back to the Geneva of the 1500s via Knox's Scotland. Be sure you know enough about our national denomination to feel comfortable, but also please know that no one of us can control all a large denomination does, any more than a single citizen can always have his/her way with the great American nation. In other words, when we join a local congregation, we also join a national denomination.

The real meaning of this question five has to do with bringing into this church family an attitude of "agreeableness," even when one disagrees with lawfully made decisions. We expect Presbyterians to differ and to disagree; we equally expect Presbyterians to seek to work cooperatively on all things and to display an agreeable spirit in the midst of disagreements.

By an affirmative answer to question five one is agreeing ahead of time to work for the common good, a theology faithful to Scripture, a holy and healthy morality, and the peaceful resolutions of differences and disagreements, without resorting to division.

By affirming these five vows of church membership, we are saying that we are Christians who seek by God's grace to live as Christians ought to live, and who seek to worship God and serve humankind faithfully and peaceably, within the context of the Presbyterian Family of Faith called the PC(USA). But it should be clear that our first and foremost commitment is to Jesus Christ, our Lord and Savior.

In the early days of the Church when being a Christian often cost one his life, those early Christian men often were recruited into Caesar's legions to fight his wars. They found that the oath of allegiance to Caesar was made by cutting the left wrist with one's dagger and from one's own blood signing his *sacramentum* (oath of allegiance) to Caesar. Christians found in this pagan ritual a model for their own allegiance to one superior to Caesar, even Jesus Christ. Therefore, these early Christians took the pagan term for "oath of allegiance" (*sacramentum*) and transformed it to describe the Christian celebration of "the Lord's Supper" or "Eucharist" in which Christians took a vow to supersede the vow to Caesar through the *sacramentum* to Christ Jesus the Lord! "Christ is greater than Caesar," they proclaimed. From that day on, in the Christian vocabulary, "sacrament" incorporated all our heartfelt allegiance to the absolute Lord of lords and King of kings, whose we are, and to whom we bow in humble service.

This describes something of the depth of convictions we Christians should have for our Lord and Savior Jesus Christ as we seek to serve Him within the family of faith into which He has brought us!

THE MECHANICS OF JOINING THIS PRESBYTERIAN CHURCH

[Note: The teacher should make clear the mechanics of joining his/her particular Presbyterian Church, if they should differ from what is described below.]

I. You May Join by Transfer of Letter

We will receive anyone into our membership by a church letter who is in good and regular standing in any evangelical church. (Letters of transfer are ordinarily available from Presbyterian (USA) and Cumberland Presbyterian churches, United Methodist churches, and Congregational (UCC) and Reformed churches.)

The church office usually writes for your church letter, receiving it directly from your former church. Should you authorize us to write for your church letter and it is not available, we then alter the church records to report "reception by reaffirmation of faith." This is one of the reasons our session asks all uniting with our church to reaffirm their five church vows.

II. You May Join by Reaffirmation of Faith

Members of denominations which do not grant letters of transfer to churches outside their own communion (such as, the Roman Catholic Church, the Orthodox family of churches, the Episcopal Church, the Baptist churches, the Church of Christ and the Christian Church, the Lutheran churches, the Bible churches, and independent and charismatic churches) are welcomed into the Presbyterian family by "reaffirmation of faith"; that is, by reaffirming those same five church vows.

This reaffirmation of faith into the Presbyterian Church is also used for those who have been inactive and wish to make a fresh beginning in the Christian life and desire to rededicate themselves to Jesus Christ without rebaptism. These persons meet with the session and, by affirming the five church vows, reclaim Jesus Christ as Savior and Lord and proclaim anew their desire to be faithful disciples in Christ's Church.

III. You May Join by Profession of Faith

We also welcome into our fellowship anyone who is willing to acknowledge Jesus Christ as his/her personal Savior and Lord; who believes in Almighty God Who has revealed Himself as Father, Son, and Holy Spirit; who promises through Bible study, prayer, participation in the Lord's Supper, worship, and the fellowship of believers to endeavor to grow in his/her faith; and who will promise to support the Church in its worship and work, peaceably, to the best of his/her ability.

Each person joining by profession of faith and who has not been baptized previously will be baptized during the reception of members, in connection with a regular Sunday worship service, usually during our New Member Recognition Service.

All new members will meet with the session and affirm or reaffirm their five church vows before the elders. (No one is received into membership in absentia.) This will be a happy time when each one is introduced and welcomed and voted into membership, pending the five "I do's."

ORIGINS AND HISTORY OF THE PRESBYTERIAN CHURCH

[Note: The teacher may wish to use this section as background reading and refer only to those parts appropriate for answering the questions raised by his/her class.]

The history of the Presbyterian Church is the same as the history of Western Christianity until the appearance of John Calvin in the early 1500s. This is not to say that there are not some traces of the particular perspectives which came to be embraced by John Calvin and his followers as far back as the early Old Testament days. It is to say that there is no separate history for Presbyterianism until the Protestant Reformation. Thus, we Presbyterians, for better or worse, must claim the history of Western Christianity and particularly that of the Roman Catholic Church as ours, until John Calvin came on the scene.

Certainly within scripture itself we Presbyterians could claim Abraham's faith in obeying a call from God to go to a land unknown, Joseph's confidence in the sovereignty and goodness of God, Jethro's wisdom in urging his son-in-law Moses to name elders to assist him in governance, Isaiah's understanding of the exceedingly heinousness of sin and the holiness of God, Jesus' teaching regarding the Father's ability to pass Him the cup of the Cross for the salvation of believing humankind, Paul's theological system of God's grace and election and sovereignty, and John's proclamation of God's ultimate victory over death, as all these are keystone building blocks of the Presbyterian belief-system.

Following the era of Jesus and the apostles, the early church struggled in a hostile world to find breathing space, persecuted by a hostile Jewish parent and a jealous Roman Empire. These early Christians, many living in the catacombs, often paid for this faith with their lives. They fought the heresies of Gnosticism and Antinomianism, the Judaizers, the Marcionites, and the Montanists. "The blood of the martyrs became the seed of the Church," as it expanded gradually and as an outlaw faith throughout the Greco-Roman world, to Africa and to parts of Asia and India.

 ca. A.D. 30—Jesus was crucified; Peter preached at Pentecost

 ca. 35—Stephen was martyred; Saul of Tarsus was converted

 ca. 46—The first General Assembly (Council of Jerusalem) was held

 ca. 96—The writing of the New Testament was completed

 150—Justin Martyr authored his *First Apology*

 230—Church structures were publicly built

 303—Diocletian began his great persecution

When Emperor Constantine in A.D. 312 became a Christian, the faith for both better and worse became legal and expanded like wildfire, though not always were the new adherents "profitable servants." The church soon became seduced with power, and for three hundred years in the time of the "Christian Empire" true believers faced great difficulties in keeping to the simple biblical faith when many sought to use the trappings of Christianity for their own glory. Augustine's *City of God* taught many concepts later adopted and supported by Presbyterians.

A.D. 312—Emperor Constantine was converted

325—First Council of Nicea was convened

381—Rome made Christianity the state religion

386—Augustine accepted Jesus Christ as Savior and Lord

405—Jerome completed the Latin Bible, the *Vulgate*

410—The Visigoths sacked Rome

440—Leo the Great was made Bishop of Rome

451—The Council of Chalcedon was convened

540—Benedict created his monastic *Rule*

When Gregory was elected Pope of Rome, the Christian Middle Ages began. Conflict was inevitable between the Christianized pagans/the paganized Christians of Rome and the barbarians of both North Africa and Central and Eastern Europe who swept into Rome itself on numerous occasions destroying all in their path. The Roman Empire eventually became the Holy Roman Empire as church and state in Rome became identical. As masses were baptized, their paganism overwhelmed biblical faith. The Holy Roman Empire sent thousands of monks as missionaries to the pagan peoples of Europe; gradually tribe after tribe accepted some kind of faith in this "Christ" and submitted to Roman authority. In these Middle Ages, called Medieval, "Christendom," with its mixtures of good and bad, Christ and Rome, church and state, paganism and faith, became a reality. Conflict became inevitable again between the weakened West (Rome) and the challenging East (Constantinople). By A.D. 1054 the East and West split became final; the churches of the West were Roman Catholic; the churches of the East were Greek Orthodox. The papacy went on to see its secular power reach its zenith. Then, reformers sought to correct the corruption of papal power, some from within the church as orders of reform, and others on the outskirts of the church such as the Waldensians, Wyclif, Hus, and Savonarola. The church had gained the world but lost its soul. The Holy Roman Empire and its Roman Catholic Church had become "the mother cesspool of immorality," as some of its own children declared, and ready for a thorough cleansing from heaven.

A.D. 590—Gregory the Great was made Pope of Rome

622—Islam was born at Mohammed's hegira

800—Charlemagne was crowned Holy Roman Emperor

988—Russia was "Christianized"

1054—The East-West split was completed

1095—The crusades began

1173—Waldensian movement, a preview of Protestantism, began

1208—Francis of Assisi forfeited his wealth for Christ's sake

1220—The Dominican Order was established

1232—The first "inquisitors" were appointed by Gregory IX

1272—Thomas Aquinas wrote his *Summa Theologiae*

1302—Papal supremacy was proclaimed by *Unam Sanctam*

1378—The great papal schism began

1380—Wyclif developed an English Bible translation

1415—John Hus was burned at the stake

1418—Thomas a Kempis wrote *The Imitation of Christ*

1453—The Eastern Roman Empire fell to Islam

1456—Gutenberg produced the first printed Bible

1479—The Spanish Inquisition was established

1497—The Church excommunicated Savonarola

1506—Work began on the new St. Peter's Cathedral in Rome for which
        money was raised over Europe by means of selling indulgences

The Reformation came to Europe on the tacks of a German Augustinian monk and priest by the name of Martin Luther, who had found true peace with God and conversion to a living Jesus Christ, not by following all the rules and stipulations of the Church, but by reading and believing what Paul had said in Romans about "justification by grace through faith." Luther discovered God's truth: faith alone, grace alone, scripture alone, Christ alone; good works were to follow Christian faith. He rejected many of the evils of his contemporary Church, including the selling of indulgences (by which the Church gained money in exchange for an alleged forgiveness or "indulgence" for a sin people wished to commit sometime in the future. This was a corruption of the concept of the grace and forgiveness of God; it was a scheme by which the medieval Church gained enormous wealth while ignoring the biblical call to all sinners to a holy life and an avoidance of sin.) Luther's tacking his ninety-five statements to the cathedral door (the bulletin board of that day) was a normal thing for anyone to do who wished to enter into public debate about a matter; he had no idea that he would thereby start the greatest religious conflict in European history and eventually be ousted from the very Church he sought to help.

Soon many in Europe joined Luther in demanding that the Church clean up its act; among these was John Calvin, a French Catholic, scholar, and law student, who began to study the Scriptures and was converted to Christ and the Reformation. A writer of one of the world's greatest systematic theologies while still in his early twenties, he was forced to flee Paris in 1534 for safety in Geneva, in which city he performed most of his ministry and did his teaching to a generation of scholars in exile from around the world, including John Knox of Scotland. He reminded the world of biblical teaching on morals and ethics, government and personal responsibility; he developed a system of theology founded on the sovereignty of God and the priest-hood of all believers; he provided the foundational concepts of republican, representative government for church and common-wealth. From Geneva Calvinism permeated life and faith in Switzerland, France, the Rhineland of Germany, Holland, Hungary, Scotland and Northern Ireland, and parts of Eastern Europe and England, and wherever their colonists settled around the world, including America, where Calvinist Puritans arrived with the first English settlers in Jamestown in 1607!

1517—Luther tacked his *Ninety-Five Theses* to the Worms Cathedral door

1518—Ulrich Zwingli moved to Zurich, Switzerland

1525—The Anabaptist Movement began

1533—In Paris John Calvin was converted to the Reformation

1534—Henry VIII separated the English Church from Rome

1536—Calvin published his *Institutes of the Christian Religion*

1540—Loyola founded the Society of Jesus (Jesuits)

1545—The Counter-Reformation was initiated by the Council of Trent

1549—The Anglican *Book of Common Prayer* was distributed

1559—John Knox arrived on his final trip to Scotland

1563—The *Thirty-Nine Articles* was first published

1611—The *King James Bible* was published

1620—The *Mayflower Compact* was written

Calvinists settled America from many sources. The Dutch, who in 1623 settled New Amsterdam (New York), were Calvinists. The French Huguenots who settled the Carolinas were Calvinists. The Pilgrims and the Puritans held different forms of Calvinism while settling New

England. Presbyterian Scots settled early in New Jersey and the Carolina coasts. Between 1705 and 1775 at least 500,000 Presbyterian Scotch-Irish came to America, primarily through Philadelphia and then settled in western Pennsylvania and Ohio and in the mountains and valleys of inland Virginia, the Carolinas, Tennessee, and Kentucky, as well as Georgia and Alabama. By the time of the American Revolution, it is said that King George (blaming the rebellion on the Presbyterians) accused damsel America of being seduced by the Presbyterian parson!

There were enough Presbyterians in America by 1706 to form a presbytery and by 1716 to form a synod. The General Assembly was convened in Philadelphia in 1788 at which time our Constitution was written and the present republican and representative form of government was approved. Some of these same authors stayed in Philadelphia for the writing of the United States Constitution the next year. There is thus a close similarity of governance principles in these two documents and kinship between Presbyterian Church government and U.S. civil government. Presbyterians expanded rapidly by immigration and outreach; at one time it appeared as though Presbyterianism might actually become the largest Protestant family of faith in America. But in 1741, in 1837, and in 1861 schism set in, crippling an otherwise growing church. Resolutions to some of these controversies were only recently settled in 1983, though even that reunion caused some other negative separation in some local environments.

1633—Galileo was forced to recant his scientific theories

1636—Harvard College was founded to provide the New World with ministers

1646—The *Westminster Confession and Catechisms* were drafted in London

1678—John Bunyan wrote *Pilgrim's Progress*

1706—The first American presbytery was founded

1729—American Presbyterians adopted the *Westminster Confession/ Catechisms* as "standard"

1732—The first Moravian missionaries were commissioned

1738—John and Charles Wesley experienced evangelical conversions

1740—The Great Awakening was at its height

1780—Robert Raikes began the modern Sunday School Movement

1788—The General Assembly of the Presbyterian Church, USA, was founded

1793—William Carey sailed for India and began the modern missionary movement

1801—American Congregationalists and Presbyterians adopted a "Plan of Union"

1807—Wilberforce led in the abolition of the slave trade

1810—In America the Cumberland Presbyterian Church was formed

1819—Channing published *Unitarian Christianity*

1827—Darby founded the Plymouth Brethren and popularized dispensationalism

1837—American Presbyterianism divided into "Old School" and "New School"

1848—Karl Marx published *Communist Manifesto*

1855—Dwight L. Moody was converted to Christ

1859—Darwin published *On the Origin of Species*

1861—The American "Old School" Presbyterian Church divided North and South

1896—Billy Sunday began his revivals

1906—In America a partial reunion between the PCUSA and the CPC took place

1910—*The Fundamentals* were published and distributed to all pastors and leaders

1925—Modernists and Fundamentalists began a forty-year battle for control of the PCUSA

1929—The PCUSA Fundamentalists lost Princeton Seminary

1949—Billy Graham began his prominent career of Crusades for Christ

1973—The ultra-conservative Presbyterian Church in America was formed

1983—Mainline Presbyterians (North and South) reunited

In spite of controversy, the Presbyterian Church has faithfully sought to spread the gospel to all parts of the world and, as 1995 General Assembly Moderator Marj Carpenter has discovered, has founded more missions in more countries than any other denomination in history. The Presbyterian Church continues to make major contributions to the worlds of education, law, science, business, government, health, and peacemaking. The Presbyterian Church offers a healthy environment in which to rear children in the Christian faith, as parents know that their children will gently be encouraged to acknowledge a faith of their own at the appropriate time, a faith that will carry them through the difficulties of life. The Presbyterian Church is open, caring, committed to Christ, faithful to the scripture, and seeks to offer the world a Savior for our sin.

THE REFORMATION AND THE
MIDDLE WAY—*VIA MEDIA*

An Outline

I. The Reformation and Presbyterianism
  A. The Renaissance
    1. Cultural Turmoil
    2. Political Turmoil
    3. Economic Changes in Western Europe
    4. Religious Change Developed into "The Reformation"
  B. The Three-Pronged Reformation (ca. 1500–1650)
    1. First Reformation of Luther (modest)
      a.) Form on European Continent: Lutheranism (1517+) (successful in Germany and the Scandinavian countries and wherever their colonists settled)
      b.) Form in England: Anglicanism (1534+)(similar in mood to Lutheranism, but not directly related to Luther in leadership or cause for development) Successful in England and throughout the former British Empire
      c.) Discarded only those things explicitly forbidden in Scripture
    2. Second Reformation of Calvin, Zwingli (moderate)
      a.) Developed more thoroughgoing Reformation (1518+) (called variously "Calvinism," "Reformed Movement," "Presbyterianism," "Puritanism")
      b.) Discarded both those things explicitly and implicitly forbidden in scripture
      c.) Successful in Switzerland; France; Hungary; Holland; Scotland; parts of Germany, England, Poland, Czechoslovakia, Romania; and in many English, Dutch, and German-speaking areas of the world
    3. Third Reformation of Anabaptists (radical)(1525+)
      a.) Radical "Left" of Reformation: Mennonites, Baptists
      b.) Rejected anything tainted with Roman Catholicism, especially "Infant Baptism" and "Covenantal Theology" and "Churchianity"
      c.) Motto: "We speak where the Bible speaks; we are silent where the Bible is silent."

      *d.)*In America in early 1800s inspired Campbellite Movement (Disciples, Christians, Church of Christ)
    4. Counter-Reformation of the Roman Catholic Church (the Council of Trent, 1545)

II. *Via Media:* The Middle Way of Presbyterianism
    A. In Polity: Congregational, **Presbyterian**, Episcopal
    B. In Liturgy: Informalism, **Blend**, Formalism
    C. In Evangelism: Mass Evangelism, **Both**, Confirmation
    D. In Theology: Fundamentalism, **Balance**, Intellectualism
    E. In Freedom: Permissiveness, **Balance**, Authoritarianism
    F. Between Individualism and Churchianity: **Balanced Covenant Concept**
    G. Between Emotionalism and Rationalism: **A Faith of both Head and Heart**
    H. Blend of the best of the Continent and of the American Frontier

III. Presbyterianism: Its History and Meaning
    A. Moses and Jethro in the Wilderness (Exodus 18:13–27)
    B. History of "Elders"
    C. *Presbuteros* is Greek for "elder"
    D. Second largest group of Protestants in the world; Lutherans are first
    E. Double Standard: Broad in respect to membership; exacting (narrow) in respect to officers
    F. Origin of "Deacon": Acts 6:1–6
    G. God's Specifications for Officership: Titus 1:5–9; 1 Timothy 3:1–7; 1 Peter 5:1–4

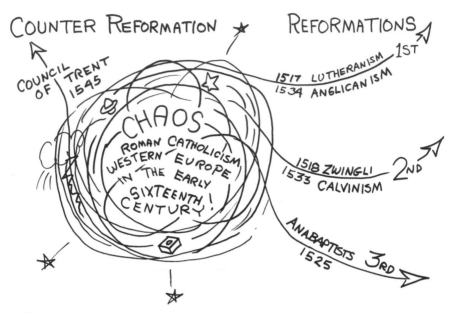

A Lecture

In the fifteenth and sixteenth centuries Western Europe arose from the deadness of the Dark Ages and threw off many of the shackles which had bound it for centuries. The Renaissance brought enlightenment in the arts, in education, in cultural revolution, and in mass change. Political turmoil brought the rise of nationalism and the sense of nationhood which marked the destruction of the Holy Roman Empire. Economic changes reintroduced the use of money, the rise of burghes and cities, the beginnings of the work ethic and the rise of a middle class, and the eventual demise of feudalism. Science was born; inquiry and learning again became respectable. With the printing press, literature was mass-produced for the scholars who multiplied and wrote and read in their native tongues as well as in the historic languages of Hebrew, Greek, and Latin. World trade expanded the West's knowledge of the earth. It is no wonder, then, that this sweeping expansion of knowledge soon troubled that ancient bastion of conservatism and what was contemporarily sometimes viewed as "the mother cesspool of immorality," the Roman Catholic Church (of that day)!

In the early sixteenth century, religiously speaking, chaos reigned in Western Europe and in the Holy Roman Empire, as religious change swept Europe as Martin Luther, John Calvin, and many others dared to challenge Rome on biblical grounds. (See the illustration on the preceding page.) Building on the witness of the early efforts for reform of the Roman Church by the Waldensians, Wyclif, Hus, Savonarola and others, the Reformation was born in 1517 and kept Europe ablaze with change and controversy for 150 years; the world has never been the same since. Though sometimes we think of the Reformation as one continuing movement, it is truer to acknowledge that there were in the main three major Reformations, each suc- ceeding upon the heels of the other, each producing a special kind of changed church.

If one assumes that the Roman Church was the "establishment" of 1517, the citadel of conservatism of that day, then the First Reformation (of Luther) was a purification which basically sought to redeem Rome or least to limit the reform to a discarding only of those things (such as indulgences) explicitly forbidden in Scripture.

This was the thrust of Luther's efforts on the continent; out of this reform came Lutheranism. If the Roman Church had given just a little, it is highly probably that Luther would have remained Roman Catholic, as that was his original intention. He was forced out of the Roman Church and only reluctantly founded a new church.

In England in 1534, King Henry VIII sought only to break the political power of Rome, not to purify its ecclesiastical teachings, though reformation also eventually took place in England too. Thus, in England arose a second variant of Luther's modest reform; this has historically been known as Anglicanism/Episcopalianism, which more often than not bears a striking resemblance to a modified Romanism.

In both cases, much of the energy of each was invested in efforts to bring change within the Roman structure; failing that, each formed a new church much akin to the former. Even today it is clear that Lutheranism and Anglicanism retain much of the flavor of a right- wing, conservative evolutionary change from the "given" Roman mode.

After Luther came John Calvin, who, in 1533, centered his reform in Geneva, and who consciously sought a more-thoroughgoing refor- mation. Calvin, supported by Zwingli, sought initially to stand with Luther in Luther's reformation; but when he could not agree with Luther on the true scriptural teaching regarding the Eucharist or the Lord's Supper, he went his own way and founded the "Reformed Movement." Calvin and his followers developed a more exacting reformation, discarding both those things explicitly forbidden in scripture and those things which could be deduced as implicitly being forbidden by scripture. Calvinism came to be known as "the Reformed Movement," "Presbyterianism," and in England "Puritanism." Calvinism significantly altered the religious map in Switzerland, France, Hungary, Holland, Scotland, in parts of Germany and England and eastern Europe, and flourished in most English-speaking and Dutch-speaking parts of the world, even up to today. Like the First Reformation, those in the Second Reformation (of Calvin and Zwingli) sought to retain the biblical concepts of "Catholic," as defining a "universal church" concept.

If modest describes the First Reformation, then moderate defines the Second Reformation. However, once the flames of change began to burn and the scriptures were turned loose freely on the people, many alternative ideas surfaced. A Third Reformation took place, not led by one person nor contained in one area nor described under any one label other than "Anabaptist"(from the Greek prefix *ana* meaning "again"). This left-wing of the Protestant Reformation turned radical and loosed all kinds of revolutionary forces and ideas. The Anabaptists rejected the concept of "universal church" or "catholic"; they rejected everything related to their former Roman attachments, including infant baptism and the covenant concept and "Churchianity." They supported only "believers' baptism" and were known as rebaptizers and cried boisterously: "We speak where the Bible speaks; we are silent where the Bible is silent." These Anabaptists produced for the world those known as Mennonites and Baptists, and, later in America, the Campbellites (Christians, Disciples of Christ, and Church of Christ) followed in their train.

Jack Rogers, formerly of Fuller Seminary, introduced me to part of the following illustrative analogy. As there were three strains of the Reformation, so there are three ways of cleaning out one's sock drawer: the Anglican/Episcopal/Lutheran way, the Presbyterian/Reformed way, and the Anabaptist/Baptist/Campbellite way.

The Anglican/Episcopal/Lutheran way is to open the sock drawer, perhaps half way, peek in, pull out those few obvious misfits and wornouts and quickly place them in the rubbish bin; one may then review the reformation, pronounce it done, close the drawer, and go about other tasks. This is reformation modestly done!

The Presbyterian/Reformed/Calvinist, on the other hand, moves to the task with dispatch and determination, completely removing the sock drawer, turning it totally upside down on the bed; this reformer places a new paper liner in the drawer and then meticulously selects only the best and most useable socks in pairs to return to this "thoroughgoingly reformed" drawer, leaving all "questionables" out for immediate discard; the job has been done; only those items of which there is no doubt have been allowed to remain. This job has been well-reformed!

Finally, the Anabaptist/Baptist/Church of Christ approaches the same task with little enthusiasm; the reformer opens the sock drawer and with disgust on his face he calls a neighbor and together they haul the entire chest of drawers out of the house to the alley for city trash pick up, for in that sock drawer there was little to reform and a great deal to discard!

More could be said of the Reformation(s). Suffice it to be said that the Protestant Reformation produced three waves of reformation, distinctly different, with our Presbyterian heritage arising out of the *via media* of Protestantism. This remains true today and explains much of who we are and why we behave as we do.

Although followers of the Second Reformation could by no means claim exclusive rights to the following seven base or fundamental statements of belief, it is true that these theological cornerstones, taken together, uniquely formed Presbyterian thought:

1. The Lord God is the Sovereign Ruler of all things, all kingdoms, all people

2. The Bible is God's Word to humankind and His "infallible rule for faith and practice"

3. All believers have direct access to God through His Son and therefore have the responsibility to serve as priests one to another

4. God calls (elects) those whom He will in the context of the Covenant Community of Faith

5. The Invisible Church of God is worldwide (catholic) in scope; breaks in the visible church obscure but do not destroy this essential unity of His Church, which is found wherever the Word is rightly preached, the Sacraments are rightly celebrated, and church discipline is rightly administered

6. The Lord Himself is the Lord of human conscience; no other human has the absolute right to dictate to another's conscience

7. There should be zeal for righteousness but moderation in all things

The people of the *via media* or middle way in every age, including our own, may be described as people ultimately orthodox in conviction and experience, but slow to force their views on others, even on other presbyters. We sense that everyone has a responsibility for his/her own views to answer to the Lord. We cringe at cutting others off. We trust God to rule and overrule, even in His Church. We may debate how to interpret scripture, but ultimately we come out with a high view of scripture and of the Faith Community, the Church. We are broad, often adopting a latitudinarian posture toward others; this means that we often allow pluralism; sometimes too much for our own good. We are ecumenical to the core, even as we hold to our Reformed views. We are committed to a search for the unity of the Church, even as we seek ever to reform (by scripture) our own Reformed Faith. We have never seen ourselves as the whole Body of Christ. We emphasize connectionalism as our way of declaring our opposition to independency. We struggle for one Reformed body per nation, which was Calvin's ideal. Even after we fight and split we are conscience-bound to attempt to reconcile and to reunite. We are never content with where we are; we always struggle to attain a greater understanding and obedience of God's truth.

Ever pulled, ever pressed between independency (power to the masses) on the one hand, and hierarchy (power to the autocratic system) on the other, we press forward with a commitment to the middle way of representative government. We are the people of the *via media*, sometimes pulling friends from both left and right, while at other times losing people to those same left/right viewpoints. We provide an easy meeting place for persons from those other Reformations, but we find ourselves on occasion facing enormous tension in the left-right pull. All of these characteristics and tensions contributed to the long struggle for American Presbyterian reunion (1861–1983).

Let us look again at the Presbyterian Way, the *via media*.

A. In polity (government) Presbyterians are between the episcopal system on the right and the congregational system on the left. Episcopacy in either the oligarchy or monarchy forms is comparable to the secular government of the few or of a king; congregationalism is the ecclesiastical form of the Greek city-state or the New England town-meeting. Presbyterianism is a republican form of government, akin to that of the United States of America, whose Constitution was greatly influenced by Presbyterians.

B. In liturgy (worship) we of the *via media* are not limited to high church formalism or low church emotionalism. We have room for heavy formalism with its read prayers; we equally are at home with informal worship with extemporaneous prayers and sermons from the heart, though well-prepared. We may or may not wear the academic gown, symbol of the teaching elder, or the clerical collar with tabs. There are few restrictions on laity's participation in worship leadership. We are a both/and blend in worship.

C. In evangelism and church growth we include room for mass evangelism and individual conversion. We normally grow our own Christians through the covenant family and the confirmation class, as young people take for themselves the vows first taken for them by their parents at their infant baptism. Yet, we also use the invitation for public profession of faith and receive many by adult profession of faith and baptism. We hold both revivals and preaching missions. We support church extension, new church development or planting, home and international missionaries, and rescue missions.

D. In theology the Presbyterian Church has always produced greater-than-normal-shares of great teachers and theologians. On the whole, we continue to be orthodox, by any standard. We are home to large numbers of fundamentalists who hold to a simple way of following the Lord of the scripture. We also welcome those who would stretch our minds, inspire us with new insights into ancient truth, and provide intellectual stimulation of God's ever greater world. Presbyterianism at its best is balanced in this area; imbalance often produces for us problems which lead to splits and troubles within the family.

E. In freedom we seek to shelter pluralism with boundaries, broad boundaries. Just where to place those boundaries often causes strife. We permit people to hold diverse views within a Presbyterian framework. We even have a dual standard, requiring one level of assent to a general Presbyterian viewpoint by our ordinands (officers) and another level, quite broad, for our ordinary church members, who must declare themselves on five—and only five—constitutional questions (acknowledgment of one's personal sin; acceptance of God's Son, Jesus Christ, as one's personal Savior and Lord; agreement to attempt to live the Christian life; promise to support the Church family in its worship and work to the best of one's ability; and agreement to submit to the government and discipline of the Presbyterian system). All ordinands (deacons, elders, and ministers) must fit themselves generally within the Presbyterian theology and polity and pass examinations (both written and oral) by governing bodies of their peers. Hence, there is within the Presbyterian system both modified authoritarianism and modified freedom. Again, we see the middle way.

F. The people of the *via media* seek a balance between individualism on the one hand and community on the other. We recognize every person as having two names: his/her given name describes one's uniqueness as an individual, created with no other copies by the heavenly Father and one who in a unique, unmatched way must be called to the Lord.

On the other hand, each has a surname, symbolic of his/her belonging to a family, a family with whom God enters into covenant. Thus, Presbyterians believe in the covenant concept and emphasize the nurturing opportunity for God's Spirit to act and call.

G. The people of the middle way seek to balance the human needs of emotionalism and rationalism. We Presbyterians seek to commit to God both our hearts and our heads. Presbyterians strongly support education for all; Presbyterians seek to help all the helpless through a strong sense of compassion.

H. History has blended into American Presbyterianism the best of the continental experience of the Calvinists and the best of the American frontier, particularly through the side history of the Cumberland Presbyterians, separate as a major body from 1810 to 1906. Among Protestants the world over we are the second largest body, with the Lutherans number one. George Gallup reports that of all religious groups in America today, we Presbyterians are the most evenly spread throughout all fifty states.

There are many obvious strengths to the heirs of the Second Reformation, not the least of which is the compatibility often furnished refugees from the First Reformation (high church people) or from the Third Reformation (low church people). In my own life I have personally been the beneficiary of such; this occurred when my English Anglican father and my American Southern Baptist mother found their greatest personal peace in service to God in the middle way of Presbyterianism.

Sam, a reserved Englishman, attended Mom's Southern Baptist services, only to find that not one, but every man, in the congregation had to greet him loudly, shake his hand and pat him on the back, a most difficult experience for such a shy fellow. Then, when the services started there were much in-church visiting and talking, endless announcements, many crying babies, a loud music director, unknown emotional music, unscripted prayers, and a spellbinder of an extemporaneous and lengthy sermon with a never-ending demand at the invitation for souls to be saved that moment, all of which conspired to make Sam a bit uncomfortable. Then, when he learned that his Anglican experience with Christ was just not acceptable to the Baptist Church, that he would have to repent of his sins (again) as though he had never been a Christian, become "a Baptist Christian," and be rebaptized by immersion, that was too much for him and quietly, but firmly, he told Lucile that he could not become a Baptist, no matter how much he loved her!

Lucile, an ardent and spirited Baptist of red hair and small stature, then determined that she and her groom would indeed worship together and form a Christian home even if she had to become an Episcopalian. Together they marched hand-in-hand the next Sunday to the Episcopal Church, where only a couple of gentleladies nodded a reluctant greeting and touched them with hands of gloved weakness. Unseen by  most, they slipped into a back pew where in near silence the service began with much kneeling and stately "collects" composed several centuries ago in King James English, heavy organ-overpowered hymns of unknown-to-Mom origin, an unenthusiastically delivered intellectual lecture which failed to call anyone that day to any action for Jesus. His church was as quiet as hers was noisy. When she was finally able to obtain answers to her questions of inquiry, she discovered that she could be accepted as an Episcopalian once she had completed a course of study and the Bishop had visited to place his hand of approval on her. This did not set well with an action-now Southern Baptist.

Both disappointed in the other's church, this couple, as they continued their courtship, found the Presbyterian Church, which had enough noise, enthusiasm, and freedom for Mom and enough quiet and form and intellectual stimulation for Dad. Two weeks after their marriage they together became Presbyterians, these refugees from the First and Third Reformations having found the Second Reformation *via media*. I would also suggest, with tongue-in-cheek, that their predestination became fulfilled that day! Thus, when the Hassall children entered this world, we were welcomed into a single-church family, ready for us to worship as a family every time the church was open; how I do thank my parents for getting together in a single church prior to our entrance into the family! That decision molded my life for Christ.

My parents found that, whereas neither could accept the vast change to the other's Christian denomination, both could serve God in the somewhat compatible environment of the Presbyterian Church. Some of you have experienced this same phenomenon.

Another advantage is Presbyterians often are the bridge people between high church and low church. I remember that meeting of the Murfreesboro (Tennessee) Ministerial Association when I, as a Presbyterian, was able to enlist in our membership on the same day two friends, the local Roman Catholic priest and a neighbor Church of Christ minister/businessman. Have you not noticed that in most ecumenical groups Presbyterians usually surface to a higher percentage of top jobs than our numbers would ordinarily allow? In all my ministry I have noticed that I, a Presbyterian minister, have been one of the few persons who could normally be welcomed into any and every home of the community, for most persons feel they can at least partially relate to me and they knew that Presbyterian ministers do not normally take advantage of such hospitality to force their views upon unwilling neighbors.

But, there is one great disadvantage to being of the middle way, a disadvantage which marks Presbyterian history as a series of explosions, troubles, and schisms. Presbyterians seek to think for

There is a disadvantage to being of the Middle Way.

themselves and normally allow for diversity of opinion within their ranks. But every once in awhile two sets of strongly held convictions, often one set influenced from the left and the other influenced from the right, clash. The middle ground becomes a battlefield instead of a meeting ground. Of all groups, the Presbyterians find the handling of such breaks the most difficult.

Baptists and other heirs of the Third Reformation with their non-centralized government divide over important issues like amoebas. The process is considered normative and occurs often enough to be survivable. Such divisions can often be healed quickly when divisive personalities leave. Such amoeba divisions have often actually become a means for reproduction and growth for such low church groups.

On the other hand, the hierarchists apparently have discovered the means to retain symbolic unity in a pope, a council of bishops, a conference, a prayer book, or a centralized governmental system, while allowing for complete diversity within the body. We note that the Roman Catholics and the Episcopalians did not split during the U.S. Civil War. Usually in such hierarchical churches all local church property is owned by the centralized governmental authority. This tends to slow down schism.

Meanwhile, Presbyterians cannot divide like amoebas nor appeal to some centralized authority above the fray. Presbyterian polity requires a modicum of conformity to objective confessions. Alternative views may be examined by groups of peers who may declare a position as unacceptable, in spite of our heritage for pluralism. Presbyterianism seems to attract "partyism"; the "in's" sometimes seek to force the "out's" out. Historically, those abandoning the Presbyterian vessel often found ways to take their property with them. Hence, the chief weakness of Presbyterianism is its inclination to split, to splinter, particularly in Scotland, America, and Korea. Presbyterians divide like splintering wood, splintering yet again. Yet, history shows that usually within three generations old wounds become new reconciliations.

ETHOS AND PERSONALITY OF THE PRESBYTERIAN CHURCH

But Joseph said to them [his brothers], "Don't be afraid. Am I in the place of God? You intended to harm me, but God intended it for good to accomplish what is now being done, the saving of many lives." (Genesis 50:19–20)

"Come now, let us reason together," says the Lord. "Though your sins are like scarlet, they shall be as white as snow; though they are red as crimson, they shall be like wool." (Isaiah 1:18)

Peter replied, "Repent and be baptized, every one of you, in the name of Jesus Christ for the forgiveness of your sins. And you will receive the gift of the Holy Spirit. The promise is for you and your children and for all who are far off—for all whom the Lord our God will call." (Acts 2:38–39)

In these three Scriptures we find clues to the emphases of Presbyterians and clues to our corporate character and personality, our "ethos" if you will.

In the Genesis reference, we Presbyterians take great consolation that there is a Sovereign Lord of the universe who has a plan and purpose for everything and makes sense out of all the chaos which surrounds us in our human existence. How good it is know that the One in whom we trust can take the worst that happens to us and bring good out of it, as Joseph discovered and as we observed with the cruel death of the innocent Jesus on the Cross! Indeed, if there is any one statement of truth which holds Presbyterians together and has become characteristic of us, it is the certainty of "the sovereignty of God" in and over human affairs.

In the Isaiah passage we find two balancing concepts which have become characteristics of those in the Presbyterian "Middle Way" family. There is first the assurance that the God who created humanity seeks "to reason" with us, to enable us to exercise our minds and to come to conclusions based on facts, and treats us (as creatures) as persons with whom He enjoys dialogue and conversation and relationship! Hence, those who check find Presbyterians particularly interested in the health of the human mind (along with education) and the exercise of reason (along with emotion) as each one discovers God and God's way for us in our life of faith and practice. Secondly, clearly emphasized here is God's concern both for the heinousness and pervasiveness of human sin along with God's delight in covering sin, burying sin, changing its nature and power over His beloved creatures who regularly fall and fail. Thus, there is a balanced reference both to the reality of human sin and the power of God's redeeming grace. Again, we see foundational Presbyterian concerns which flower in our character.

In the Acts quotation from Peter's sermon at Pentecost we not only hear the clarion call for repentance (a Presbyterian emphasis) but also an assurance of the acceptance of sinners by Jesus Christ, of the promise of forgiveness, and of the certain gift of the Holy Spirit. We also hear Peter's plea that believers and their children be baptized and enjoy the promise of God. This promise of God (the covenant of the Old Testament now expanded by the death and resurrection of Jesus Christ) is not only for believers but for their children, not only for Jews but also for Gentiles ("those that are far off"). Although there are gratefully some of Jewish extraction who attend our classes, most of us are Gentiles from the peoples who "are far off." Let us thank God for His expansive love to include us too in His plans.

Ethos is defined as "the distinguishing character or tone of a . . . religious group." Presbyterians, like all families of faith or denominations, have special characteristics which cluster among family members. I would propose that much of what is discovered to be characteristics which compose our unique ethos or personality arise out of two parallel sources: our place in history as heirs of the Second Reformation or the *via media* and our special Reformed theology. Just as the birth order of children within a family seems to have major influence on the developing characteristics of children when they become adults, so does our place in the development of the Protestant Reformation.

One will generally find Presbyterians open to ideas from both left and right, high and low church, more formal and less formal, continental and American frontier, power flow from the top and power flow from the bottom, and able to relate positively both with fundamentalists and rationalists, and with colleagues from the Orthodox, Roman, Anglican, Lutheran, Anabaptist, Independent, and Bible Church traditions. Openness and variety characterize Presbyterianism.

The following series of words or phrases captures much of the tone of this "People of the Middle Way": "Reformed," "Calvinistic," "Presbyterian," "Connectionalism," and "*Via Media.*"

We hold what is called a "Reformed Theology," which is especially defined by its essential tenets with which we will deal in the next chapter (though most of these theological ideas have already come to our attention in the wording of the Five Church Vows we have previously reviewed in detail).

"Calvinistic" refers to our specific heritage arising out of the teachings and practice of John Calvin, as he emphasized the authority of scripture, God's sovereignty over all of life, human sin, God's grace, God's initiative, the power of the Cross, God's steadfastness, the priesthood of all believers, orderliness over chaos, involvement of the people in the governance of the Church, and the need to educate the mind, and to do all human vocation as unto God.

"Presbyterian" refers especially to "the rule of church life by lay elders and ministers" (both of which bear the Greek label for "elder," which is *presbyter*), elected by the people and functioning in an orderly and graded series of governing bodies for the common good.

"Connectionalism" is the Presbyterian way of saying that, although we reject for our own use any hierarchical system (which places power at the top where such power simply flows down eventually to the people in a trickle-down design) or any congregational system (which may place all persons voting on all matters at all times, irrespective of their spiritual maturity and responsibility, and which may degenerate into a rule by mob), we firmly believe Christians are more effective and more biblical when we connect with each other and do not seek to live in isolation from each other. We reject the idea of an isolated Christian, for it seems to deny the valued *koinonia* or "fellowship of the saints," so highly lifted up in scripture.

Via media Presbyterianism may be well and accurately defined by this series of seven couplets:

- a Biblical/Evangelical People

- a Reasonable/Moderate People

- an Ecumenical/Inclusive People

- a Compassionate/Caring People

- a Negotiating/Process People

- a Studying/Thinking People

- an Orthodox/Confessional People

Presbyterians of all perspectives claim the Bible as their authority. Presbyterians of all viewpoints declare good news for humankind; that is one meaning of evangelical. So, in a sense, all Presbyterians can reasonably claim to be both biblical and evangelical. However, it must also be pointed out that most Presbyterians in the studies discovered by the Presbyterian Panel, which is a Presbyterian Gallup Poll, are indeed biblical and evangelical in the more traditional sense of holding a high view of scripture as the trustworthy Word of God and adhering to the essential uniqueness of God's only way of salvation through God's grace for sinful humanity in the atonement of Jesus Christ on the Cross.

By our history and by our theology, Presbyterians have been led to place major emphasis on the value of human learning and competency in education for all. Presbyterians require their ministers to have graduate school educations and prove competent in human learning as well as in their theological studies. Presbyterians have always sought to found academies, colleges, and seminaries that all may know who God is and what God has provided humankind in the way of knowledge of our environment. The health and the use of the mind are critical to Presbyterians.

Being the middle child of the Reformation, Presbyterians found early that our views were "in-between" views, considered by many as too moderate. We would not be pressed into mediocrity nor into either a partial and lackadaisical reformation nor into a radical gangbusters all-or-nothing extremism. From our birth as a movement until today, it still is our nature to seek compromise, the middle road, the "let's all work together" approach. We therefore major on peacemaking, at least most of the time. Hence, a significant part of our self-image is that we are indeed reasonable and moderate people.

The Middle Child

As a people who intentionally claim to be only a part of God's Church, it became incumbent upon us to reach out to others who are a legitimate part of God's Church; that includes all who truly believe in God's revelation of Himself as Trinity and who trust in God's incarnate Son as Savior from our sins and Lord of our lives. With these views foundational it is an easy matter to reach out to others who claim the name of Christ in fellowship and acceptance. Thus, Presbyterians accept the baptism of all other Christians when such baptism is done in the trinitarian name of God and with water. Presbyterians accept the prior Christian experience and membership from most churches who claim Christ (there are questions about some few who appear to be more cultic than scriptural). Presbyterians have been in the forefront of almost all ecumenical movements. Presbyterians open our membership to all kinds of repentant sinners. Presbyterians generally have an open-arms policy towards other Christians around the world. We are ecumenical; we are inclusive.

Presbyterians, as Calvinists, are activists in almost all arenas of human need. We can be found in almost any trouble spot of the world, in almost any natural disaster or outbreak of disease. We care for the hurting and the dying in almost every environment. When we err, we tend to err in offering too much help or help in the wrong way, but we seldom err by having an uncaring spirit. Every General Assembly speaks as though it has authority in resolutions to solve most of the world's ills or conflicts that year; we sometimes know what we are doing. We always have the heart and the zeal; we do not always have the facts or the best solutions. But no one can accuse this People of the Middle Way of not caring, of not being compassionate.

John Calvin was trained in law and forensics, and much of his life he was both cleric and city manager. From that day to this those trained in law and in process seem very comfortable among Presbyterians. Our system of government does not allow us to acquiesce in the decisions made on high nor to agree to the demands of the throngs. Instead, we must negotiate, compromise, deal, perfect the nuances of language, and follow the process of legislation. Thus, we have a highly political heritage which requires us to perfect both the skills of negotiation and process. No wonder we make good leaders in business and government!

Our Latin motto is *Ecclesia Reformata, Semper Reformanda, Secundum Verbum Dei* which means that we Presbyterians believe God has called us to be "The Church reformed, always reforming, according to the Word of God" and the call of the Spirit. (This is vastly different from the erroneous view of some that we are to "change and always be changing.") The difference, of course, is the phrase "by the Word of God and the call of the Spirit." In practice, this motto requires Presbyterians ever to be willing to review what Scripture says about any subject again. We must be willing to study and restudy again the same subjects, believing as we do that the Teacher of the Scripture, the Holy Spirit, does not contradict Himself but theoretically may have yet more to say to believing hearts and listening ears out of the same revealed Word of God available for centuries. Thus, we Presbyterians seek ever to be a studying people and a thinking people, using our God-given brains to go with our God-redeemed hearts.

Someone has said that if one throws a cat into the air, it will always land on its feet; since I have never tried this exercise, I will take this statement as truth. But, I do know that no matter how odd or unorthodox Presbyterians may appear at times, when all is said and done, we Presbyterians, like the cat, land on solid ground on orthodox feet. Our systems often move slowly, but they do move surely. God's way is ultimately discovered and supported by most Presbyterians most of the time. We also are a family of faith who writes down our convictions; indeed, we have a whole book of such written convictions, called "confessions, statements, creeds, catechisms, and declarations" which our ordinands must support in their ordination vows. Thus, the Presbyterian faith is not only orthodox (in the usual meaning of that word), but we are also confessional, meaning "true to our written statements of faith."

This People of the Middle Way are grace-filled, open, and inviting of you, the seeker, to discover Jesus Christ and walk with them in faith as they seek together to love and serve our Lord and Savior Jesus Christ. Welcome to the family!

THE PRESBYTERIAN BELIEF SYSTEM

One excellent way to discover the Presbyterian belief system is to review carefully all the theological presuppositions contained within the questions used as the Five Church Vows, as we have done. May I suggest five other avenues which may also provide insight into this goal.

Let us see what a brief review of "the five points of classic Calvinism," known as "TULIP," will teach us. Over four hundred years old, these are not broadly used today, but they do provide significant information regarding Presbyterian theological roots.

The *Book of Order* in its ordination vows provides an ordering by priority for spiritual authority which can save Presbyterian believers much grief and heartache by knowing who has top authority and what should draw our suspicions, lest we be entrapped by a Jim Jones or a David Koresh.

A review of the ten "essential tenets of Reformed faith," as identified by our *Book of Order*, helps us understand what is uniformly important to those who hold a Presbyterian and Reformed theological perspective. Such a brief overview will give the inquirer insight into the psyche of the People of the Middle Way.

In my personal experience of trying to understand Presbyterian theology and to explain Presbyterian beliefs to newcomers to the faith, the tract, "The Presbyterian Church: Its Beliefs," by Ernest Trice Thompson has been the most helpful; it is reprinted for the help it can offer to others in their search.

For those who want just a statement about the main difference between the Presbyterian Church and a specific other denomination, the reprinted article, "The Reformed Faith. . . . What Is It?" from *The Presbyterian Journal*, has proved of much assistance.

Five Points of Classic Calvinism—TULIP

T otal depravity teaches that all humankind is helpless before God due to human sin, which is resident in all areas and compartments of every human life. This doctrine does not hold that each person is as bad as he/she can be, but rather that all of us are infected with sin in every area of our lives. Thus, we humans utterly need God's intervention to save us from ourselves and our own choices.

U nconditional election declares that, no matter how we human beings get involved in the process of eternal salvation, clearly "God's choice of the sinner, not the sinner's choice of Christ, is the ultimate cause of salvation."* God is the only eligible voter in this election of eternity. How thankful we are that He chose us—and that not of our doing but out of His grace and for our serving!

L imited atonement denotes that the Cross of Calvary was adequate to cover the penalty due for the sins of those whom God in Christ determined to save. Its further teaching that the Cross was efficacious for those saved, and them alone, is less accepted by today's Presbyterians than these other teachings.

I rresistible grace declares that God's grace never fails and is therefore invincible. God in Christ through the Holy Spirit "graciously causes the elect sinner to cooperate, to believe, to repent, to come freely and willingly to Christ."** God's goodness fulfills His desire to save those whom He has chosen.

P erseverance of the saints is a theological way of saying that God never loses those who are His. He is always faithful and does not and will not let those who are His children slip out of His hand; His patience in loving us to the end is beyond understanding but such a joy for those who experience this assurance of salvation.

---

* David N. Steele and Curtis C. Thomas, *The Five Points of Calvinism Defined, Defended, Documented*, Presbyterian and Reformed Publishing Co., Philadelphia, 1963, p. 17.
** Ibid., p.18.

Rank of Spiritual Authorities Over Life

Primary authority is Jesus Christ, the Living Word.

Secondary authority is the Bible, the Written Word, as revealed through the Holy Spirit.

Tertiary authority is the "essential tenets of the Reformed Faith," as found in our Presbyterian *Book of Confessions*.

Fourth level authority is the combined testimony and experience of the Church, especially as determined by actions and statements of governing bodies.

Lowest level authority is the private understanding and personal experience of the individual Christian.

We Presbyterians recognize that the primary authority for us in all our faith and life is Jesus Christ Himself, God's Living Word, as we discover Him in scripture and by the informing power of the Holy Spirit. The Lord Jesus Christ himself is our chief authority, to whom our secondary authority, the Bible, God's Written Word, bears witness.

However, there are many times when we must look beyond Jesus himself and the Holy Scriptures to discover what must be interpolated from divine revelation. When we seek this level of inquiry, we acknowledge we are heeding a tertiary level of authority and do the best we can to comprehend the mind of the Church, as contained in the historic creeds of the Church over time. Often what we seek is not available through the Lord Himself, nor Holy Scripture, nor the creeds of the Church, so we turn to the wisdom and statements of contemporary Church governing bodies and believers; we sometimes find such fourth level authority among sermons, position papers, and other utterances which seem to have group wisdom of contemporary fellow believers.

The least trustworthy and most dangerous authority is self-authority; we must be ever aware of the possibility of self-deceit, either by private opinion ("I am right; the rest of the world is wrong") or by personal experience, which, of all platforms of truth, is the shakiest and least sturdy, for experience can be misinterpreted and embellished for personal gain and benefit. Wise Presbyterians do not trust their unique insights nor their unique experiences. We test every private opinion and every personal experience by the Living Word, the Written Word, the creeds of the Church, and the perspective of the contemporary Christian family of faith.

Essential Tenets of the Reformed Faith

The Reformed Faith has certain characteristics and convictions without which it cannot exist; in other words, these convictions are essential for it to be what it claims to be; these necessary convictions are identified as ten essential tenets. These are identified in our *Book of Order*, G-2.0300-G.2.0500.

The first two we share with Christians everywhere and in all time; thus, they are drawn from the "faith of the Church catholic": "the mystery of the triune God" and "the incarnation of the eternal Word of God in Jesus Christ."

1. Trinity
2. Incarnation

The next two we share with those who also were a part of the sixteenth century renewal of the Church: that is, from the "faith of the Protestant Reformation"; "the rediscovery of God's grace in Jesus Christ as revealed in the scriptures"; and "grace alone, faith alone, scripture alone."

3. Justification by grace through faith
4. Scripture is the Word of God

The remaining six tenets are our family characteristics; as a family we hold the following from the faith of the Reformed tradition:

Central to this tradition is the affirmation of the majesty, holiness, and providence of God who creates, sustains, rules, and redeems the world in the freedom of sovereign righteousness and love. . . . [O]ther great themes of the Reformed tradition [include]: (1) The election of the people of God for service as well as for salvation; (2) Covenant life marked by a disciplined concern for order in the Church according to the Word of God; (3) A faithful stewardship that shuns ostentation and seeks proper use of the gifts of God's creation; (4) The recognition of the human tendency to idolatry and tyranny, which calls the people of God to work for the transformation of society by seeking justice and living in obedience to the Word of God.*

5. Sovereignty of God
6. Election
7. God's involvement in the covenant community
8. Stewardship of our resources and the earth
9. Sins of idolatry and tyranny
10. Commitment to justice and obedience

"THE PRESBYTERIAN CHURCH: ITS BELIEFS"
Ernest Trice Thompson

The Presbyterian Church has definite beliefs, drawn directly from the Word of God, which are stated clearly.

It holds the common Christian faith and cooperates fully with all other Christian people. Some of its important beliefs are summarized briefly in the paragraphs that follow:

God—God, the Creator of the heaven and the earth (Genesis 1:1) is sovereign Lord of the universe (Daniel 4:35). He has revealed himself partially through nature and fully in the Bible. His supreme revelation of himself is in Jesus Christ. God is righteous in all his ways, loving in all his dealings (2 Peter 3:9).

Man/[woman]—Man/[woman] is a sinner, unable to save himself/(herself), and therefore needs a Savior (Genesis 6:5–6; Romans 3:19–23; Romans 6:23a).

Christ—God, out of his great love, provided a Savior (John 3:16–17). This one and only Savior is the Lord Jesus Christ, God's own Son, born of a woman, and is therefore God and man, and as such is able to make reconciliation between God and man/(woman) (Romans 3:24–26).

Salvation—For our sin Christ died on the Cross, taking upon himself our guilt and the penalty of sin that we might be forgiven and set free (Romans 5:8; 8:1).

---

* PC(USA) *Book of Order*, G-2.0500a.

Faith—Salvation comes to us only through our faith in Jesus Christ as Savior and Lord (Romans 6:23; Ephesians 2:8–9; John 1:12; John 3:14–15; Acts 16:30–31; Hebrews 7:25).

Repentance—Repentance from sin, which is more than sorrow for sin, is a turning away from sin unto newness of life in Christ (Mark 1:14–15; Acts 2:37–38; Matthew 3:8).

The Holy Spirit—The Holy Spirit leads to conviction of sin, to repentance and faith, and to a desire for a new life, and so brings about the new birth without which no man/(woman) can enter into the kingdom of heaven; and He enables us to die more and more unto sin and to live more and more unto righteousness (John 3:3–8; John 16:7–13).

The Bible—The Bible is the inspired and authoritative Word of God (2 Peter 1:19–21; 2 Timothy 3:16).

The Organized Church—The organized church is a divine institution for the worship of God, the propagation of the faith, and the mutual comfort and strength of those who believe (Matthew 16:16–18; Ephesians 5:23–27).

The Sacraments—There are only two of these holy ordinances instituted by Christ, wherein by outward signs, inward spiritual meanings and graces are conveyed to sincere participants—worthy receivers.

> *Baptism*—Water baptism, a symbol of spiritual baptism, is the rite of entrance into the church; it is to be administered to all who believe in Christ and to their children as a token that they are members of the household of God (Acts 16:14–15; Ephesians 6:4; Acts 16:32–33).
>
> *The Lord's Supper*—This is a memorial of Christ's life and death and coming again (1 Corinthians 11:23–26).

A Public Confession of Christ as Savior—A public confession of Christ as Savior is made by joining the church (Matthew 10:32).

The Lord's Day—The first day of the week is the Christian Sabbath for public worship. After the resurrection of Christ the disciples met for prayer and worship on the first day of the week (1 Corinthians 16:1–2; John 20:19–26).

Christian Responsibility for Witnessing for Christ—A Christian has the responsibility of witnessing for Christ, and so helping to build up a human society permeated by the spirit of Christ (Acts 1:8; John 1:34–42; 2 Corinthians 3:2–3).

The Bodily Resurrection of Christ—The resurrection of Christ was a bodily resurrection. There will also be a bodily resurrection of all men/[women] and recognition in life to come (1 Corinthians 15:3–4, 20–23; John 14:1–3).

The Second Coming of Christ—The second coming of Christ will be personal and glorious. It is ours to watch and work and be ready when He comes (Matthew 24:42–44).

The Final Judgment—There will be final judgment with Christ as the Judge; and there will be eternal blessedness for all those who in this life accept Jesus Christ as Savior and seek to follow Him as their Lord (Acts 10:42; Hebrews 9:27; 2 Corinthians 5:10).

"REFORMED FAITH . . . WHAT IS IT?"
(Copied from The Presbyterian Journal, *October 4, 1972)*

A thoughtful church member asked her pastor: "What is the *Reformed Faith* to which you so frequently refer? I hear much of the *distinctives of the Reformed Faith* without a clear indication as to what those distinctives are."

Below is a paraphrase of the answer the pastor gave:

The Reformed Christian believes that he/she is justified by faith in Jesus Christ through the immediate work of the Holy Spirit in his/her heart, hence he/she is *not a Roman Catholic.*

The Reformed Christian believes in the Trinity, therefore, in the full deity of the Lord Jesus Christ, so he/she is *not a Unitarian.*

The Reformed Christian believes in the sacraments and the Word of God as means of grace, so he/she is *not a Quaker.*

The Reformed Christian believes in a prior work of God's grace in the human heart leading to salvation, and in the predestination of all things according to God's sovereignty, so he/she *isn't a Methodist.*

The Reformed Christian believes that the priesthood of all believers has replaced a special priesthood, and that ordination is by the Holy Spirit and not by any power granted in human succession, so he/she *isn't an Episcopalian.*

The Reformed Christian believes that baptism represents the coming of the Holy Spirit upon the believer, and that the promise is to believers and to their children who are also heirs of the covenant, so he/she *isn't a Baptist.*

The Reformed Christian believes in a representative government rather than a purely democratic government, so he/she *isn't a Congregationalist.*

In addition to these denominational distinctives, *the Reformed Christian* bases his/her relation to God and his/her hope of salvation on the gospel of the Lord Jesus Christ, incarnate Son of God, crucified for our sins, raised for our justification, reigning in the hearts of His people by the Holy Spirit and coming again in time to judge the quick and the dead.

He/she also believes in the fellowship of believers on earth and in fruitful Christian living.

Thinking like a Presbyterian.

"THINKING LIKE A PRESBYTERIAN"

Many years ago Joseph Gettys provided the PCUS with an invaluable booklet, *Meet Your Church*, to encourage inquirers into Presbyterian membership. One particular chapter, "Thinking Like a Presbyterian," made a significant impression on me and a few of its major ideas cannot be improved upon and deserve passing on to a new generation of would-be Presbyterians. I hold that there is a distinct Presbyterian way of seeing life; this Presbyterian character is formed by our theology, our history, and our ethos. It is an honorable way of enjoying faith and pleasantly serving the Lord.

We "**start [our] thinking with the Bible as [our] guide**." Whatever is the challenge before us, whatever we seek to do in life, whatever problem lies before us, we Presbyterians find it a natural habit early on to turn to scripture to discover what God says which may be of help to us in our time of challenge, confusion, or crisis. We understand that God's Holy Spirit is ever seeking to teach us what God's will is for our circumstances; scripture is His first means of communicating with us.

We know instinctively that God is in charge, that God already knows what is happening and what the conclusion will be, and that God will bring good out of it, no matter how bad it may initially appear from our human viewpoint. We know our first and foremost task in this life is "to glorify God and to enjoy Him forever." We continue "**thinking with God at the center of life**." This keeps us from becoming self-centered or focused on our own problems, sins, or failures. When we know the Father is the captain of the vessel, the sea storms seem less frightening. When we remember that the Creator of the universe is our own personal "Abba," "Daddy," then we fear even the worst devils and fiercest creatures no more. We have been gifted with the comforting assurance that we are held in the hollow of His hand, that He cares for us. What joy to know that "in life and in death we belong to God" and that "with believers in every time and place, we rejoice that nothing in life or in death can separate us from the love of God in Christ Jesus our Lord!"

As we Presbyterian believers journey through life, we are reminded that we are to "**keep Christ and the Holy Spirit as living realities**." We know God's mercy, but we experience Him firsthand through Jesus Christ; later we come to know God as the Comforter, the shy person of the Trinity, who never calls attention to Himself but always seeks to place the spotlight on Jesus. Presbyterians do not easily go off on tangents into "Jesus Only" or "Holy Ghost" extremes; we simply daily plod along happily knowing that God, the Triune One, wants us to have no wobbles in our balanced relationship with the Trinity. We know that Jesus saves us and that the Holy Spirit is personal, present, and empowering us daily for God's good and glory.

As we live, it is important to Presbyterians to remember that in this life we can never become perfect; nor are we called to be "Messiah" to any one else. Thus, we seek to "**keep sin and salvation in [our] doctrine of redemption**." Sin is not simply a past dragon once slain; sin is a nipping dog at our heels, alive and far too active in our lives. We Presbyterians know we never outgrow temptation and can always fall, so we attempt to cultivate a humble spirit both about our own potential for renewed failure and our neighbor's imperfections. However, we seek to keep ever before our eyes the assurance of God's salvation in Jesus Christ, who on the tree did redeem unworthy folk like ourselves! Friends, this is both a healthy and a humble theological reality.

Presbyterians know our salvation comes from the Lord, that He took the initiative, that we are saved by His grace through our faith (which He provided). We have been taught the difference between what is the root of faith (salvation) and what is the fruit of faith (our good works). Therefore, we find it necessary to "**keep the proper relationship between faith and works**." Having been saved by His grace, we know our task is to produce for His glory a garden of the fruit of good works and pleasant blessings for others, all that the Father may be honored!

As maturing Presbyterian Christians, we have come to understand how important it is to worship God regularly both at home and in the sanctuary and to offer Him the gift of service to our fellow human beings, especially to those less fortunate than we. Thus, we do seek to **"keep worship and work as spiritual twins**." We have discovered that the best place ordinarily for Christians to grow is in God's Church; we remember to "**keep the Church as the instrument of God**" here on earth meant for our good and maturity in Christ.

PRESBYTERIAN *CONFESSIONS*

Presbyterians, like most Christians in church history, have found it exceedingly helpful to put our theology in writing and to support and adopt creeds and confessions (statements of faith) of Christians in other eras and places, if those meet scriptural standards. Thus, we Presbyterians have affirmed a book full of confessions, creeds, and catechisms from many ages and peoples. These are published and available for study in our *Book of Confessions*, a volume to which our ordinands (officers) must affirm support; ordinary members have no obligation to be led or guided by these, though the theology found in this book will appear in many sermons and in most of the suppositions underlying what is said and done in a Presbyterian church. Thus, in the Presbyterian Church, confessions indirectly impact the congregation, rather than directly. However, often portions of such will appear as affirmations of faith within our worship services. By such statements of faith the church declares to its members and to the world who and what it is, what it believes, and what it resolves to do.

Within our *Book of Confessions* there are currently eleven documents. Below is a brief summary of each, its date, name, occasion, and key issues:

The Nicene Creed of the fourth century sought to clarify for all time certain key doctrines dealing with the person and work of Jesus Christ and the nature of the Trinity. It was the result of a conference called by the newly converted Roman Emperor Constantine who sought to reduce religious bickering and to develop a unified Christian Church to bring greater cohesion to his Roman Empire.

The Apostles' Creed, the shortest document and the most popular, reflects second century baptismal statements, though all the ideas contained herein may be found in the sermons recorded in the New Testament. Actually formalized in the fifth century, the name indicates its intention to proclaim what the apostles themselves taught respecting the essentials regarding the Triune God and basic Christian dogma.

The Scots Confession of 1560 reflects the views of John Knox, who had recently returned from training in Geneva under John Calvin, in his efforts to lead Scotland out of the Romanism of Queen Mary and into the Protestant Reformation. This lengthy statement sought to clarify the biblical teachings its authors believed the Roman Church had rejected or misunderstood. It has special importance to Presbyterians.

The Heidelberg Catechism of 1563 reflects its German origin and its combined Lutheran and Reformed heritage. Requested by Freiderich III, the two Swiss reformers who authored this catechism (a question-and-answer rote memory method of learning) sought to lay out in plain language (for that day) the practical meaning of this reformed faith to daily living. There is a joy, a gratitude, and an uplifting spirit which still win modern supporters for its winsome theology and inspiring style.

In 1566 the Swiss Reformed Churches developed the *Second Helvetic Confession*, which provided much clarification in a confused day, especially about the Church and about the Christian experience of believers. Originally written as a personal statement of faith by Heinrich Bullinger, Zwingli's son-in-law and successor, this lengthy document noted both what to support and what to reject, biblically speaking.

The Westminster Confession and its sister documents, *The Larger Catechism* and *The Shorter Catechism*, were the results of four years of scholarly work by pious leaders in England in 1643–1646 as they daily gathered in Westminster Abbey, having been commissioned to develop a unifying faith-document for the Protestants of the British Isles by the Long Parliament. These doctrinal statements sought to deal systematically with the whole of Christian theology, basing its work on a strong commitment to scripture, a high view of the sovereignty of God, and God's call to humankind through His covenant. These have proven to be the most influential creeds upon American Presbyterianism; as a boy I was privileged to obtain my personal theology by memorizing the Westminster Shorter Catechism. For serious Presbyterians I highly recommend Westminster and its magnificent teaching about Christian responsibility.

In 1934 *The Theological Declaration of Barmen* defied the Nazis and declared that these German Christians were prepared to die to put Jesus Christ before Hitler. The format was to declare what its authors supported and what they rejected as false doctrine or wicked actions.

Following the civil rights movement and anarchy in parts of America *The Confession of 1967* sought to explicate the theme and duty of reconciliation in a badly divided America. This modern creed, greatly influenced by neo-orthodoxy, caused much conflict and dissension before it was finally adopted by a then-liberal United Presbyterian Church in the United States of America, a product of a reunion between Northern Presbyterians and a branch of Scot Presbyterians in 1958.

A Brief Statement of Faith, adopted in 1991 by the PC(U.S.A.), was a promised by-product of the 1983 reunion between the Northern Presbyterians (UPCUSA) and the Southern Presbyterians (PCUS), which formed the PC(USA). It seeks, in a few lines, to provide an overview of contemporary Presbyterian faith which is both faithful to the ten essential tenets of Reformed Faith and inclusive of newer theological insights from scripture. It does not cover all theological bases and does not claim to be comprehensive.

In the ensuing pages we quote the text of this last confession and by boldfacing note at least ten biblical ideas new to confessions as well as list the line numbers where the essential tenets may be found. As a member of the final writing team for this confession, I have strong convictions that this statement is both true to scripture and true to where Presbyterians are today in their theology. An oral reading leaves one feeling the faith, the power, and the integrity of those holding such views in a world of uncertainty, moral confusion, and human need.

The most important word everyone on earth must hear from *A Brief Statement of Faith* is "Yet" found in line 40—"*Yet* God acts with justice and mercy to redeem creation." This is the "Good News" that in spite of sin and condemnation, God loves God's creatures, including you and me! This is the heart of the Presbyterian understanding of faith!

A BRIEF STATEMENT OF FAITH (1991) PRESBYTERIAN CHURCH (U.S.A.)

1   In life and in death we belong to God.
2   Through the grace of our Lord Jesus Christ,
3   the love of God,
4   and the communion of the Holy Spirit,
5   we trust in the one triune God, the Holy One of Israel,
6   whom alone we worship and serve.

7   We trust in Jesus Christ,
8   **fully human, fully God**.
9   Jesus **proclaimed** the reign of God:
10   **preaching** good news to the poor
11   and release to the captives,
12   **teaching** by word and deed
13   and **blessing the children**,
14   **healing** the sick
15   and binding up the brokenhearted,
16   **eating** with outcasts,
17   **forgiving** sinners,
18   and **calling** all to repent and believe the gospel.
19 Unjustly condemned for blasphemy and sedition,
20 Jesus was crucified,
21   suffering the depths of human pain
22   and giving His life for the sins of the world.
23 God raised this Jesus from the dead,
24   vindicating His sinless life,
25   breaking the power of sin and evil,
26   delivering us from death to life eternal.

27 We trust in God,
28   whom Jesus called Abba, Father.
29 In sovereign love God created the world good
30   and **makes everyone equally in God's image**,
31   **male and female, of every race and people**
32   **to live as one community**.
33 But we rebel against God; **we hide from our Creator**.

34	Ignoring God's commandments,
35	we violate the image of God in others and ourselves,
36	accept lies as truth,
37	exploit neighbor and nature,
38	and **threaten death to the planet entrusted to our care**.
39	We deserve God's condemnation.
40	Yet God acts with justice and mercy to redeem creation.
41	In everlasting love,
42	the God of Abraham **and Sarah** chose a covenant people
43	to bless all families of the earth.
44	Hearing their cry,
45	God delivered the children of Israel
46	from the house of bondage.
47	Loving us still,
48	God makes us heirs with Christ of the covenant.
49	**Like a mother who will not forsake her nursing child,**
50	like a father who runs to welcome the prodigal home,
51	God is faithful still.
52	We trust in God the Holy Spirit,
53	everywhere the giver and renewer of life.
54	The Spirit justifies us by grace through faith,
55	**sets us free to accept ourselves** and to love God and neighbor,
56	and binds us together with all believers
57	in the one body of Christ, the Church.
58	The same Spirit
59	who inspired the prophets and apostles
60	rules our faith and life in Christ through Scripture,
61	engages us through the Word proclaimed,
62	claims us in the waters of baptism,
63	feeds us with the bread of life and the cup of salvation,
64	and **calls women** and men to all ministries of the Church.
65	In a broken and fearful world
66	the Spirit gives us courage
67	to pray without ceasing,
68	to witness among all peoples to Christ as Lord and Savior,
69	**to unmask idolatries in Church and culture,**
70	**to hear the voices of peoples long silenced,**
71	**and to work with others for justice, freedom, and peace**.

72   In gratitude to God, empowered by the Spirit,
73   we strive to serve Christ in our daily tasks
74   and to live holy and joyful lives,
75   even as we watch for God's new heaven and new earth,
76   praying, "Come, Lord Jesus!"

77 With believers in every time and place,
78   we rejoice that nothing in life or in death
79   can separate us from the love of God in Christ Jesus our Lord.

80 Glory be to the Father, and to the Son, and to the Holy Spirit. Amen.*

Location (By Line) of "Essential Tenets"

Trinity	5–6, 7, 27, 52
Incarnation	8
Justification	54
Scripture	58–61
Sovereignty	29, 40
Election	41–43
Covenant	47–48
Stewardship	37–38
Sin	33–38
Obedience	69–71, 73–74

* Instead of saying this line, congregations may wish to sing a version of the "Gloria."

Response Time

[Note: The following Intention Form and use of Response Time are suggestions; please continue the class as best meets your needs.]

First, please complete your Intention Form to enable us to know what to expect of you and your potential new membership tomorrow.

Second, please turn over to the back side of your Intention Form and list, for answer in the next class, questions you still have about Presbyterianism: how or why to join, its origins and history, its ethos and personality, its belief system, its practices, its programs. In other words, what do you yet need to know?

Third, now please give these cards to your host, who will collect them and turn them in for action and answer later when we meet.

Intention Form

Response: (please check each blank, as needed)

_____Yes, I am/we are ready to unite with (Name) Presbyterian Church.

_____I am/we are as yet unsure about uniting with (Name) Presbyterian Church. Please give me/us more time.

_____Please call to arrange a meeting for a time for questions and answers.

_____No, I/we do not wish at this time to pursue membership at (Local Church).

_____Plan on my/our joining (Date) with the class at (Time) in (Location) as the session meets.

_____Please call and let's talk about an alternative date for my/our joining (Local Church).

Signed:_____ Phone:_____(Please Print)

Address:_____

_____

Small Group Discussion

[Note: The following use of Small Group Discussion time is a suggestion; please continue the class as best meets your needs.]

Please circle up in your small groups and take a few minutes to discuss your questions with each other and with your host.

You may also want to discuss these additional questions:

1. What have you liked about this New Member Class so far?
2. How could this New Member Class have been improved?
3. What more do you want to learn about Presbyterianism?

Class Questions Answered

[Note: It is recommended that early in the fifth or sixth hour the teacher take the written questions of the class (previously turned in) and summarize and consolidate them and give the best succinct and fair answers to as many as time allows, knowing that at these points the pupils itch and need scratching.]

How Presbyterians Govern Themselves

The church word for governance or church government is "polity," which comes from the same family of words as "politics" and "policy." The way a group of Christians, gathered into a church, function and rule themselves says much about their basic theology and influences what they believe and how they live.

Presbyterians put a great deal of effort into their understanding of scripture regarding government and how we interconnect with one another. Presbyterians believe our form of government is biblical, but by this statement we do not hold that all other forms of government are non-biblical. In fact, as we read scripture, we also find elements of and suggestions supporting the other two major families of church government.

Presbyterians have sought to build our form of government or polity on seven principles for which we find biblical support:

1. Christ alone is head of the Church; all others are subordinate to Christ. Elected representatives seek first to represent Jesus Christ and only secondarily their constituents

2. Scripture alone provides Christians with authority and responsibility one for another, but no one form of government is mandated for all by scripture

3. All believers equally are to serve as priests for each other; there is no hierarchy of spiritual power except that which honors Christ and upholds the responsibility of every believer for one another

4. All church power must be administered "decently and in order" to give God glory

5. The unity of the Church is best seen as an interconnectedness or connectionalism through representative assemblies, the larger with oversight over the smaller, rather than through a hierarchy or through mass democratic rule

6. Under God, the people, gathered in congregation, have the right to elect their own leadership, including pastor(s) and elders and deacons

7. There must be a parity of ministry among the elected leaders; in our case, this is seen as parity between lay elders and teaching elders, called "Ministers of Word and Sacrament"

It is important for new members to know that when they join a particular local church congregation, they are also uniting with both their national denomination and the church universal. Thus, membership is three-fold. All who join this particular Presbyterian local church are also joining the Presbyterian Church (U.S.A.); all who trust in Jesus Christ as Savior and Lord also belong to His church universal.

Three Basic Forms of Polity

There is the Episcopal form. This is hierarchical, in which all power flows from top to bottom. (If power were water, this form would best be illustrated by the waterfall.) This theory is that God the Holy Spirit speaks to and gives power to those at the top, who then distribute power in a kind of "trickle-down" theory. There are two major illustrations of this form of government. There is the monarchical and the oligarchical.

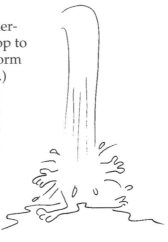

Episcopal

The monarchical sub-form concentrates power in the leader or single person at the top. In civil government this may be a king or dictator; in religious government we see this form in the Roman Catholic Church with its pope.

In the oligarchical sub-form, power is found "in the few" at the top. In civil government this could be observed in rule by a council or a court or even by a political party; when it is by three the name might be "a troika"; in religious government this form is best illustrated by the Episcopal Church with its Council of Bishops.

The second kind of government is the Congregational form, which assumes that all power by the Holy Spirit originates at the bottom or among the masses of democracy. (Again if power were water, in this form power would flow like a powerful fountain thrusting gushing water upwards.) Every member theoretically votes on every issue. There are few illustrations of such government functioning for lengthy periods of time in the civil realm, but we do have historically the Greek city-states and the New England town meetings. In the religious realm this form of government is the trademark of the Congregational Church and the Baptist Church, among others. Over time there

Congregational

appears to be a tendency for a pure democracy to come under the authority of some strong indigenous leader who overrules all the rest.

The Middle Way within polity is the Presbyterian form with its republican and representative characteristics. In the civil realm we see this governmental theory in our own United States government; in the religious arena this form is found in the Reformed and Presbyterian Churches. This polity lies in between the previously described two; this is of all polity forms the most complicated. Within the Presbyterian system we believe the Holy Spirit first gives power and authority to the people gathered in congregation to elect their own leadership; the congregation chooses to become affiliated with the larger Presbyterian body. The congregation elects its elders and minister(s) who serve as their representatives and form a church governing body called a session to make all important decisions for that local church. Presbyterians from all the sessions and churches within a region form a regional governing body called a presbytery to make all important decisions for that region. Presbyterians from all the presbyteries and churches within several states form both a larger regional governing body called synod and with all presbyteries and churches within the nation form the national governing body called the General Assembly (see the map on the following page). (Again, if power were water, the best illustration for how the Presbyterian representative polity works would be an automated "holy car wash," with water (power) coming from every direction.)

Presbyterian

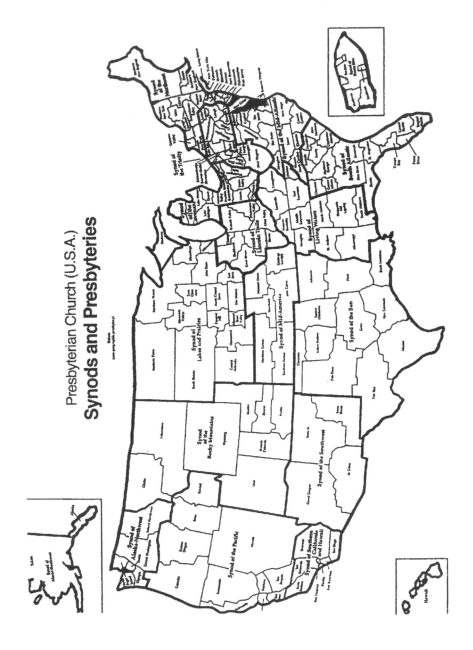

Presbyterian Church (U.S.A.)
Synods and Presbyteries

How Presbyterians Worship and Do Mission

Worship

Presbyterian worship is informed by the first question/answer of *The Westminster Shorter Catechism*: "What is the chief end of man/(woman)?" "Man's/(Woman's) chief end is to glorify God and to enjoy Him forever." We seek primarily to give to God rather than to get from God. We know our definition as human beings comes from God, not the other way around. "Worship" involves human understanding that God is worthy of our devotion and adoration; we bow down before Him and Him alone. Thus, worship is acknowledging the greater worth or value of God in comparison to human worth.

The PC(U.S.A.) *Book of Order* (W-1.1001) provides this definition:

> Christian worship joyfully ascribes all praise and honor, glory and power to the triune God. In worship the people of God acknowledge God present in the world and in their lives. As they respond to God's claim and redemptive action in Jesus Christ, believers are transformed and renewed. In worship the faithful offer themselves to God and are equipped for God's service in the world.

Presbyterians go to church to join in corporate worship. This means we go into the sanctuary not simply to get something out of it to take home to help me this week, but to glorify God! The Presbyterian goes to worship to give self back to God in praise, in prayer, in hearing the Word of God in scripture and sermon, in psalm and song, and in leaving the sanctuary to serve God in obedience as we seek to do His will where we live.

The choir's chief purpose is to lead the congregation in singing praise to God, not to perform and gain accolades for themselves, though we do value good music and gifted musicians.

Presbyterians follow the "free" tradition. Although we have stated orders of worship, none is required. Although we have access to a lectionary listing of suggested texts for sermons over time, use is not mandated. In most worship matters there is a Presbyterian way of doing things "decently and in order," which, when followed, puts into practice our Presbyterian theology. Although in some of our more continentally influenced areas, we have available clerics, clerical collars, and various clerical robes, all use is optional and local. In my experience, which has been heavily influenced by the American frontier, most Presbyterian ministers have chosen to wear pulpit robes (of the Genevan or academic style) for preaching and street clothes for everything else.

The *Book of Order* provides a section called "The Directory for Worship," which gives instruction as to worship forms and reasons for these. Yet, the use of these in Presbyterian worship, for the most part, is highly recommended, but often not required. Theology must be observed and some forms must be followed, but there remains a great deal of freedom in worship leadership. Yet, having said this about freedom and options, most Presbyterians feel more comfortable if worship is preplanned and bulletins with orders of service are available and followed.

For the new member from a non-Presbyterian background, I would recommend a few items for immediate memorization: *The Apostles' Creed*, which is the standard said affirmation of faith, the Lord's Prayer (using "debts"/"debtors" instead of "trespasses"/ "trespassers"), the Doxology ("Praise God from whom all blessings flow. . . ." and the Gloria Patri ("Glory be to the Father, and to the Son, and to the Holy Ghost. . . ."), as all of these are regularly used and are generally known by most worshipers in a Presbyterian Church. Knowing these will make you feel more comfortable over time; you will sense you belong. I also encourage you to gain familiarity with *The Presbyterian Hymnal*, becoming able to find hymns and worship helps quickly.

Stewardship

Historically, Presbyterians are conscientious workers, following Calvin's work ethic, and generous givers, knowing that all things belong to God and that "we are not our own; we have been bought with a price." Stewardship, which is recognizing that what we have in resources is but on loan from God and is not our own, is another given in the Presbyterian's road of endeavoring to grow and mature in Christ.

We maturing Presbyterians seek to serve God as good stewards in five areas:

1. We seek to discover that place in God's work where our gifts and interests match a need for "God-service"; this can be teaching for some, feeding the hungry for others, or in dozens of volunteer places of service at church for God and His kingdom.

2. Presbyterians do not leave our God at the door as we leave the sanctuary on Sundays; we seek to obey God and follow His values and ethics in our own workaday world, where we

Stewardship through daily work

seek to do our vocational work as a Christian would do it. This often alters the decisions we make, the ethics we demonstrate, the way we "do business," and what we say to and about other people. There are no standards higher than God's standards for our particular during-the-week vocation. We endeavor to give to God a good accounting of how we do business in our unique world of work.

3. Presbyterians almost always do a superior job in their chosen vocations and by demonstrating this Calvinistic work-ethic attain good wages and promotions and more than enough financial resources to care for our own needs. We remember that the Bible teaches the cheerful return to God of the tithe (10 percent) and the opportunity to give more than that to God's church and to those in special need. Thus, growing Presbyterians seek to become tithers of income as quickly as possible.

Let me tell you of Dad's learning to be a tither in the early years of World War II. Sam and Lucile, my parents, had become Presbyterians in 1931; I was born into their home in 1933, at the nadir of the Great Depression. Life was not affluent growing up in this new Presbyterian home; we knew we were broke, we did not know we were poor. World War II came along; food rationing cut the standard of living of most families; we raised our food in the victory garden and in the chicken yard. Mom made all the clothes for the three boys, who knew we were fortunate to wear good homemade "hand-me-downs." In this situation in 1943 Sam came to believe that God would have him tithe. He followed "the Belmont plan," by which he would notch up his giving level one percent every three months, if we had been able to survive the previous three months. Every time this "notching-up" worked; not once did we go hungry. We had everything we had to have; Sam was able to give God and the church a little more! This is how Sam learned to tithe.

My story is very different, though I too learned to tithe in 1943, a year marked for this eleven-year-old by memories of three good things: (a) I got my first paying job—

cutting grass for a dollar; (b) I starting my lifetime hobby of collecting stamps; and (c) I started tithing that first dollar earned. Dad also taught me the value of a college education in the course of my turning that first dollar into dimes—the first dime went to God and the church; the next two dimes went into buying "war stamps" for investing in my college education; the remaining dimes could then be spent on "up-keep," which included postage stamps, ice cream, and other dreams of a young boy. But, Dad taught me the value of tithing and saving,

Stewardship through church-giving and tithing

two lessons which continue to bless me this day. (I also still enjoy spending a bit on stamps every now and again.)

4. Presbyterians have access not only to our daily wages or salary and current income, but we also have received enormous blessings from God in accumulated wealth. Thus, we find here another opportunity to serve as good stewards of God, as we intentionally plan with our estate advisors for at least a tenth of our estate after we die to go to support God's work in this world and to meet human need. Let our wills and estate planning also reflect how serious we are about following our Lord in a complete pattern of good stewardship. To this end, many

Stewardship through estate planning

Stewardship through living better on less

congregations have estate planning assistance available to believers free simply for the asking.

5. It should be obvious that Presbyterian Christians in their endeavor to live "as becomes the followers of Christ" must care for their family, their extended family, in adequate ways, knowing that under God we are responsible for our own. (It is amazing how much better we sometimes can do on the remaining 85 percent to 90 percent of a tithed income than we were able to do when we kept most of it for ourselves.) This form of good stewardship includes not only providing financially for our total family as is needed, but also for making sure that we do not do for others what they can and must do for themselves. In other words, we avoid spoiling our children, giving them too many worldly goods, and not enough opportunities to provide for themselves. This too is a part of good stewardship from a Presbyterian perspective.

Sacraments

Presbyterians, like Protestants the world over, hold there are but two sacraments, believing that a sacrament is an instruction from Jesus Christ to all His followers in which He commanded us to do a particular action (a sign which is visible for all to see) which has a deep hidden and invisible spiritual reality. Only baptism and Communion, or the Eucharist, fulfill this definition, in our view.

A. The Lord's Supper or Eucharist or Communion. There are at least four ways to view the Lord's Supper:

1. The Roman Catholic Church teaches "transubstantiation." This view holds that the elements of bread and wine actually become the body and blood of our Lord Jesus Christ, even though these changes remain unseen and unproven by science. This is a faith view. It also alters the way we handle the elements, view the Supper, and conduct our life around what comes then to be known as "the mass." It seems to some that Jesus is re-crucified in every mass. Presbyterians do not hold this view.

2. The Lutheran Church has altered this view a bit, but from our Reformed viewpoint, not enough. Lutherans teach and hold a view of the Communion called "consubstantiation." This view agrees that science cannot trace the alterations in the elements of bread and wine, but nevertheless such real changes do occur alongside the spiritual presence of Jesus Christ. This spiritual presence of Jesus Christ is quite different from the Roman view and is akin to the Reformed view; the stumbling block is the first part of this faith-statement; namely, that the elements are indeed changed into the real body and blood of our Lord. Thus, Presbyterians do not hold this view either. Presbyterians also open Communion reception to all believers in Christ.

3. A third view is generally held by the Anabaptists and their descendants: the Baptists, many Independents, many of the Campbellites, and Bible churches. This view rejects not only the Roman view and the Lutheran view, but also the Reformed view(to be described momentarily); this view holds that the Eucharist is to be viewed primarily as "an ordinance," a "memorial," an "anniversary," so to speak, of the Last Supper. Its primary purpose is to remind the believer of something that once happened and that Jesus will come again, as He promised. In some of these congregations this is celebrated something like a family meal, to which only members of that family may participate.

4. The Reformed view of the Lord's Supper is neither high church (Roman Catholic and Lutheran) nor low church (Anabaptist). Rather, Reformed theology does not claim that the elements of bread and wine become in any actual physical sense the body and blood of our Lord. Instead, we believe that there are two unique things which happen at this celebration. First, there is the special spiritual presence

of Jesus Christ in and among the elements but especially in the hearts of the believing participants (this is different from the presence of Jesus Christ regularly through the work of the Holy Spirit). Second, we believe that the elements are vital and real reminders of the brokenness of His body and the loss of His blood for us sinners. Thus, we see and feel the real presence of Jesus Christ as we partake and sense the real price of His crucifixion (broken body and shed blood) as we see, handle, and taste the elements of bread and wine through which this reality becomes known to us uniquely.

Reformed view of the Lord's Supper

B. Baptism. There are at least three views of baptism:

1. There is the view called baptismal regeneration, by which adherents teach that baptism is God's initiation of persons into His Church in such a way that the action of baptism so-to-speak almost guarantees them a place in God's kingdom. This view is taught by the Roman Catholic Church and held by most Episcopalians and some Lutherans and Methodists and a few Presbyterians. This view identifies the outward action and timing of baptism with an eternal relationship with Jesus Christ. Some who experience baptism with this kind of theology seem to deny the need for any kind of additional personal relationship with Jesus Christ. In other words, in practice, a baptized relationship with the Church takes the place of any need for a personal relationship with Jesus Christ. Those who hold these views usually baptize by pouring or sprinkling.

2. A second viewpoint regarding baptism is that called believer's baptism, held by all who count the Anabaptists as their spiritual forebears. This view categorically denies any validity to any baptism of infants or children under the "age of understanding." In this view

baptism is reserved only for those who can knowledgeably choose to follow Jesus Christ; this limits candidates to older children, youth, and adults. Hence, it is called believer's baptism. Usually adherents of this view perform all their baptisms in the more dramatic way of immersing candidates, even those who in other traditions had already received baptism by sprinkling or pouring.

3. The third view is held by most Presbyterians and many Lutherans and Methodists. This is called covenant baptism, which may be administered both to believers and to their children, usually by sprinkling or pouring. In this view (the Reformed view) God's family is identified as being

composed of believers and their children. These children are then baptized as infants as an initiation into the family of God; their parents take their faith vows for them and promise to train them in the faith. However, each of these children must, upon reaching the age of understanding, discover what was earlier done for them by their parents; they must be confirmed in that personal faith, making that faith now their own. Salvation, then, is not tied to the act of baptism; it is tied to the faith of the believer, either a present faith or a future faith, as our God knows the future and is not (like we) tied to the present. Salvation is tied to God's action and God's gift of grace

Reformed view of baptism

by which we discover faith and profess it; salvation is not tied to a human action of placing water on one's head. This is true whether we are talking about adults or infants, for salvation is never automatic. We would encourage you to hold this view of baptism.

Presbyterians accept the baptism of all other Christians, if such has been done with water and in the name of the Father, the Son, and the Holy Spirit.

Presbyterians hold that baptism should only be done once. It is the Holy Spirit who validates baptism, not the amount of water nor the age of the one baptized. Baptism is not a repeatable sacrament, while the Lord's Supper should be repeated frequently, especially when there is a need for a personal rededication to Jesus Christ.

Presbyterians believe that baptism of children is the New Testament way of including the children of believers, just as in the Old Testament there was the ritual of circumcision, which was used to incorporate the (male) children of believers into the family of God. We are grateful that in the New Testament the way was opened to include the female children of believers into the household of faith. Thus, we see baptism taking the place of circumcision, just as the Eucharist took the place in the New Testament of Passover.

Doing Mission

Scripture provides ample mandate for mission:

> Then Jesus came to them and said, "All authority in heaven and on earth has been given to me. Therefore go and make disciples of all nations, baptizing them in the name of the Father and of the Son and of the Holy Spirit, and teaching them to obey everything I have commanded you. And surely I am with you always, to the very end of the age." (Matthew 28:18–20)

> [Jesus] said to them: ". . . But you will receive power when the Holy Spirit comes on you; and you will be my witnesses in Jerusalem, and in all Judea and Samaria, and to the ends of the earth." (Acts 1:7–8)

> [Jesus said:] "Then the King will say to those on his right, 'Come, you who are blessed by my Father; take your inheritance, the kingdom prepared for you since the creation of the world. For I was hungry and you gave me something to eat, I was thirsty and you gave me something to drink, I was a stranger and you invited me in, I needed clothes and you clothed me, I was sick and you looked after me, I was in prison and you came to visit me.' Then the righteous will answer him, 'Lord, when did we . . . ?' The King will reply, 'I tell you the truth, whatever you did for one of the least of these brothers of mine, you did for me.'" (Matthew 25:34–37a, 40)

The Presbyterian Church (U.S.A.) has carefully developed our mission description in the *Book of Order* (G-3.0300-3.0400):

> The Church is called to tell the good news of salvation by the grace of God through faith in Jesus Christ as the only Savior and Lord, proclaiming in Word and Sacrament. . . .

The Church is called to present the claims of Jesus Christ, leading persons to repentance, acceptance of Him as Savior and Lord, and new life as His disciples.

The Church is called to be Christ's faithful evangelist. . . .

The Church is called to undertake this mission even at the risk of losing its life, trusting in God alone as the author and giver of life, sharing the gospel, and doing those deeds in the world that point beyond themselves to the new reality in Christ.

Every Presbyterian congregation should have discovered its particular mission in its community. No one church can do everything that needs to be done, but all should be doing something.

As we look at how Presbyterians do mission, let us note that we have a biblical mandate to enter into the mission of proclamation of the saving grace of God in Jesus Christ to a lost world; we have a biblical mandate to provide missions of compassion and education, of policy change and of advocacy for the poor and voiceless in a lost, hurting, and poor world.

We need to provide the hurt and dying with medical missions, the hungry and ill-clothed and homeless with missions of food and clothing

and housing. There is a call to share our resources, both financial and human power, on the international, national, and local fronts. There is need to fight famine and war, ethnic cleansing and aggression. There are special needs for the unemployed, the homeless, dysfunctional families, families of prisoners, illegal immigrants, and persons with AIDS.

[Note: Here the teacher should list a sampling of the mission

efforts of his/her particular local congregation, so that prospective new members will have a sense of what this congregation believes its mission for Christ in the world today really is. See appendix A, page 105, for a sample "Description of the Mission Practice" of this local church.]

It is not enough to have a mandate for mission, a mission description of what mission ought to look like, and a methodology by which some fulfill that mission. We have something that needs the gifts and energy and resources of every new member.

Therefore, it is now essential that each member discover what God has in store for him/her to do for His glory. We start this discovery process by seeing what gifts we possess, what needs are available, where, and when, and with whom we may allow God to put us into His slot for service. This process of "letting go and letting God" do His will with us is both exciting and scary, but God in His sovereignty already has prepared us for His place of service to His people in the mission "that has our name on it."

YOUR LOCAL CHURCH: ITS HISTORY, CHARACTER, MINISTRY, MISSION, AND YOUR FUTURE PART IN IT

The teacher should present a concise, clear presentation of the history of this particular local congregation, including not only the highlights of the church's past life, but also something of its unique character, ministries, mission understanding, and intentionally describe how any new members may quickly become a part of this church's positive future. See appendix D, pages 108–111, for a sample church history used at this local church.

Lay Witness Sharing

It is recommended that at this point in the course the teacher invite a lay member of the church to give a personal witness to the potential members. To be included in a five- or ten-minute statement should be: (1) a description as to when/where/how the lay witness first came to know personally Jesus Christ as Savior and Lord; (2) how and why he/she came to membership in this particular church; and (3) how this church has assisted him/her in Christian maturity and service over time.

Guest Speakers

At this point in the course it works well to invite a limited number of special speakers from the local church membership and staff (where possible) to speak in short three- to five-minute segments about particular areas of ministry or opportunities for nurture or service or worship. See appendix B, page 106, for a sample list of guest speakers for this local church.

Materials in File Folders

As part of the teaching for this last hour, it is recommended that each student be provided a file folder with church materials included for easy reference both by the guest speakers and by the teacher. A church bulletin, a copy of a church paper (if there is one), a copy of the church budget, and other promotional pieces would be most appropriate. See appendix C, page 107, for a sample list of materials for distribution through the file folders used at this local church.

Mission Statement

If your particular congregation has a mission statement, it would be appropriate to share it with this class in an attractive way, emphasizing what your church is all about. See appendix E, page 112, for the Mission Statement of this local church.

Staff Directory/Flow Chart and Lists of Church Officers

If your particular congregation has a Staff Directory and/or a Staff Flow Chart and/or Lists of Church Officers, these should be shared with the class in this last hour as a resource to assist them to know and understand how this church works.

How To Plug In Effectively, Quickly, and Reasonably with Reward

Answers To Commonly Asked Questions

We have found that a compact list of answers to commonly asked questions is appreciated by our prospects and inquirers. Each teacher needs to customize the list for each particular church. The following are subjects for the list used at this local church:

Office Hours	Flowers
Using Church Facilities	Church Budget Pledges
Seating Capacity	Memorials, Endowments,
Ticket Sales	Stock, and Trust Funds
Weddings	Mailing Lists
Funerals	

See appendix F, pages 113–114, for the form this section takes at this local church.

The Creed of a Faithful Member

A faithful member accepts Christ's call to be involved responsibly in the ministry of his Church. Such involvement includes

- Proclaiming the good news

- Taking part in the common life and worship of a particular church

- Praying and studying scripture and the faith of the Christian Church

- Supporting the work of the Church through the giving of money, time, and talents

- Participating in the governing responsibilities of the Church

- Demonstrating a new quality of life within and through the Church

- Responding to God's activity in the world through service to others

- Living responsibly in the personal, family, vocational, political, cultural, and social relationships of life

- Working in the world for peace, justice, freedom, and human fulfillment

—from PC(USA) *Book of Order*, G-5.0102

Small Group Time:
Plugging into Your Local Church

Name:_____ Ph._____ H. _____W.
Host Name:_____ Ph._____ H. _____W.
(Fill out with a pen and turn in to your host.)

1. What first attracted you to this church? _____
_____

2. Many new members have been attending and are already involved in this church. Are you already involved with a group or in a service area?_____If so, which_____
_____

3. Do you know other people here at church?_____Who?_____
_____

4. What would be your choice for your next step of involvement? [Note: Teacher, add your own.]

_____Ushering	_____Presbyterian Women's Circle
_____Food Service	_____New Member Hosting
_____Prayer Room Service	_____Men's Bible Study Group
_____Choir	_____Teach Sunday School
_____Feeding the Hungry	_____Join Sunday School Class
_____"Habitat for Humanity"	_____Other:_____
_____A Fellowship Group	_____Other:_____
_____Other:_____	_____Other:_____

5. What did you enjoy doing in your last church and/or community?____
_____

6. What might you now enjoy doing here in your new church?_____
_____

7. Which words best describe YOU? (check two or three items)
I most like to:

___Care/Protect	___Plan/Administer	___Learn
___Show Compassion	___Pray/Intercede	___Help/Serve
___Build-up the Church	___Step Out in Faith	___Lead/Vision
___Give/Share Resources	___Encourage/Motivate	___Teach
___Provide Hospitality	___Experience Cross-cultural Life	

Class Evaluation Form

1. What was the best part of this course for you?_____
_____
_____
_____

2. What else would you have liked to have had included?_____
_____
_____

3. What was disappointing to you?_____
_____
_____

4. How do you feel this experience could be improved?_____
_____
_____
_____

5. What do you believe was the most important thing you learned? _____
_____
_____
_____

6. What attracted you to this local Presbyterian church? _____
_____
_____
_____

7. Were you invited by someone?_____By whom?_____
_____

8. Please comment on the class schedule. Was this the best way to offer you a six-hour course of study, given your schedule?__
_____
_____

Appendices

Material Used by
Highland Park Presbyterian Church [HPPC]
Dallas, Texas

DESCRIPTION OF THE MISSION PRACTICE

Some of the methods by which some churches do missions included the following found in our local church:

> assistance to the unemployed; "Habitat for Humanity" home-building; support for children's homes; assistance in matching funds for grants to small churches with capital building or repair needs; clothes closet for missionaries; emergency financial assistance for both persons within the church family and mendicants from without; financial assistance and persons to serve food at the intercity "Stewpot Ministry"; short-term mission projects in Ireland, Jamaica, Yucatan, and Mendenhall, Mississippi; Mainero (Mexico) hospital; Alaskan Eskimo witness project across Bering Strait to Siberian Eskimos; "Adopt-a-School" intercity project for remedial and tutorial assistance to children; new church developments in Las Colinas, Allen, San Juan (PR), Africa, and Trans-Amazon Brazil; international students ministry; strengthening the Presbyterian "wee kirks" (very tiny churches); "Followers" visiting and witnessing; Stephens Ministry of care; prayer room ministry; and work with senior citizens and Boy Scouts. In addition this congregation gives away through its missions program funding to support missionaries and missions on every continent where Presbyterians work.

GUEST SPEAKERS

"What Makes for an Effective Church Member"
"Meet and Mingle Time"
International Student Ministry
"Adopt-a-School" Intercity Tutorial Project
"Habitat for Humanity" Housing Project
"Presbyterian Women" Opportunities
"Nurture at HPPC"
"Stewardship at HPPC"
"Worship at HPPC"
"Serving at HPPC"

Materials in File Folder

Weekly Church Bulletin
"Witness for Biblical Morality" Sessional Resolution
Letter from Presbyterian Women
"A Place to Grow"—List of Sunday School Class Opportunities
HPPC—The Volunteer Ministry
Announcement about "Spiritual Gifts" Course
HPPC Church Budget
HPPC "First Fruits" Pledge Card
The Meyercord Library
"Highland Park Presbyterian Weekly"

CHURCH HISTORY, CHARACTER, MINISTRY, MISSION, AND YOUR PART IN IT

In the years just before the beginning of World War I Vanderbilt University in Nashville, Tennessee, was taken over by those who wished to make that school something other than the primary training school of ministers of the Methodist Episcopal Church, South. This action caused the Methodist Episcopal Church, South, to search for a new school as their primary seminary for the training of their ministers. This led to the foundation of a new school in rural Dallas County, Texas, some six miles north of the city by the Methodists who called their new college ambitiously Southern Methodist University. A village of students, professors, and administrators began to grow up around the new school on Hillcrest Avenue. Soon the town of University Park grew and eventually connected with the previously existent village of Highland Park. This growing community needed churches.

In January of 1926 the Presbyterian Extension Board of Dallas was formed to secure new locations to build Southern Presbyterian churches. By April of 1926 fifty-four people had signed a petition requesting that the board establish a Presbyterian Church in what was then North Dallas in the area which is today known as "the Park Cities." One month later, 190 people indicated a desire to join Highland Park Presbyterian Church as charter members.

It is claimed that most of our charter members came from our "mother church," which was First Presbyterian Church of Dallas. Part of the story behind that, we are told, is that Dr. William Anderson, pastor of First Church in the mid-twenties, was giving strong backing to the newly founded Dallas Theological Seminary (DTS). This school, with its dispensationalist teaching, was not universally approved by

108

the membership at First Church. Thus, some took this founding of a new church to be the occasion to leave and to move in a "more Presbyterian direction." Since DTS was considered ultra-conservative, one might then assume that some of the founders of Highland Park Church were more liberal than the fellow members they left behind at First Church.

Now back to the story. Not wasting any time, by July of that same year the current church property was found and purchased. The congregation met at the local high school (now McCullough Middle School) until August 12, 1928, when the first service was held in the newly constructed building. That first sanctuary is still extant and is in daily use, hidden in the larger overall design of our current church facilities. (Your homework this week is to locate and identify where that first sanctuary is located. Hint: the building still has the original cupola on the roof.)

The current sanctuary, which holds 1,100 people, was completed in 1941, just before Pearl Harbor, at a time when the church membership numbered 1,677. In 1950 a large two-story wing was completed to house the Christian education and fellowship areas. In 1964 the Christian education space was doubled by more building. The last major building extension was finished in 1980 with the addition of the Hunt Building, which consists of a large fellowship hall with kitchen, many adult classrooms, most of the church office space, the adult church library, and a gymnasium.

Through the years, changes in the number of Sunday worship services have been necessitated by the fluctuations in membership. Then, in 1951, the system of identical Sunday morning services at 9:30 A.M. and 11:00 A.M. was introduced. In 1954 this arrangement was extended to the Sunday School. In October of 1966 a third worship service in Wynne Chapel on Sundays 8:15–9:00 A.M. was added. From 1983 to 1992 a third identical sanctuary service was held at the 8:00–9:00 A.M. hour.

In its years of service for the kingdom, Highland Park Presbyterian Church has had only five senior ministers. From 1927–1932 the Reverend W. A. Alexander was the pastor. The church grew from 239 to 752 members. In 1932 Dr. Thomas W. Currie Sr. began to commute from Austin, Texas, where he was president of Austin Seminary, to handle the preaching and pastoral duties. The church also added our first associate pastor in 1932 who took up on-site duties in Dr. Currie's absence. From 1932 until Dr. Currie resigned the pulpit in 1937, the church grew from 792 to 1,050 members. From 1938 until 1942, Dr. Henry W. DuBose pastored the church; the church continued to grow from 1,050 to 1,944 members.

Dr. William M. Elliott Jr. was called in 1944 to Highland Park Presbyterian Church as the senior minister. By 1967 the ordained staff had been increased to five. When he retired in 1973, the church had grown from 2,141 members to approximately 6,200. Dr. Elliott's long tenure gave this congregation stability and maturity as it became the largest Presbyterian congregation in America and hosted the General Assembly. Dr. Elliott also served the PCUS as General Assembly moderator one year and headed the foreign mission enterprise for many years as the elected chair of that agency. Dr. Elliott also led Highland Park Church into national prominence as "a cathedral church" to which many over the nation looked for renewal encouragement and theological balance in a time of shifting sands.

Soon after the retirement of Dr. Elliott, HPPC called Dr. B. Clayton Bell Sr. as the senior minister. Dr. Bell was born of famous medical missionaries in China and brought with him the gift of national leadership in the more conservative wing of American Presbyterianism. In addition to the innovative leadership he provided HPPC in the way of music excellence, an expanded Christian education ministry, a new family counseling center, greatly expanded child care for members whenever they served the church, and a multitude of new and expanded programs which sought to meet the expanding needs of the people of the community. Dr. Bell is known for his sturdy biblical sermons which assist worshipers in their daily Christian living and for his national leadership of the evangelical renewal movement sweeping through first the PCUS and now the PC(USA), as well as for his leadership of the many publishing ministries of *Christianity Today* magazine.

Under Dr. Bell's leadership from 1973 to 1991 the HPPC church membership grew to approximately 8,300 members with an ordained staff of fifteen ministers. In 1990 HPPC entered into a major internal debate over the question of remaining in denominational affiliation with the PC(USA) or moving to "another Reformed body." Although the issues were complex, Dr. Bell gave leadership to those who would reform the PC(USA) rather than leave it. All but one of the ministerial staff supported him, as did 60 percent of the session and 45 percent of the diaconate. "Article XIII," the agreement within the 1983 "Plan of Union" between the PCUS and the UPCUSA, which brought about the union of the Northern and Southern Presbyterian Churches to form the PC(USA), required a two-thirds vote to "disaffiliate" with the PC(USA). After sixteen months of heated debate and grievous disputation, the congregation voted 45 percent to stay with the PC(USA) and 55 percent to move to "another Reformed body." As this vote was neither a vote of confidence in the PC(USA) and the local administration nor was it adequate to propel HPPC with its property into another affiliation, most of those who had opposed the PC(USA) affiliation left HPPC either in lump sum to found the Park Cities Presbyterian Church (affiliated with the PCA) or piecemeal to other less controverted congregations or simply dropped out of any church. This sad exhibit greatly altered the continuing scene at HPPC. We saw membership decline to about 5,000; we had to cancel one of the Sunday morning sanctuary services, and we saw the loss of about half of our Christian education program, including many classes and numerous faithful church workers and lifetime friends.

In the last four years those members who remained, plus the many new members who have chosen to place their spiritual welfare with us, have grown spiritually, have discovered new leaders with new gifts, and have continued receiving new members at a rate of about 300 plus per year. This pruned congregation is now moving into some carefully thought-out refining of mission and methodology and soon will be announcing the NOW emphasis of seeking to recruit every member in nurture—outreach—worship opportunities. In 1995 HPPC has 5,400 members, an annual church budget of approximately $5,000,000, of which $1,000,000 is invested in God's mission beyond HPPC locally, nationally, or internationally. The ordained staff now numbers ten; there are approximately sixty other staff persons serving the Lord and this congregation. HPPC continues to offer the finest Christian education program, great music, faithful preaching, two growing schools, a wonderful recreation program, a vital family counseling program, as well as continued national leadership in the conservative and evangelical renewal movements within the PC(USA).

The history of Highland Park Presbyterian Church has not yet concluded, for there is room among us for YOU! We invite you to step into this history flow and help write the future.

MISSION STATEMENT

The Mission of Highland Park Presbyterian Church
is to glorify God and enjoy Him by:

- Worshiping
- Proclaiming and spreading the good news of God's saving grace in Jesus Christ
- Nurturing the congregation through education, fellowship, and compassion
- Ministering to the community and the world in the name of Jesus Christ and through the power of the Holy Spirit
- Being a responsible member of the Presbyterian Church (U.S.A.)

Answers to Commonly Asked Questions

Office Hours are Monday through Friday, 8:30 A.M. to 5:00 P.M. Due to the many meetings and activities held in the church, the building is open until 9:30 P.M., except on Saturdays and holidays. The church operator telephone number is 526-7457; the church automated attendant number is 526-1766 plus the correct extension number. The church fax number is 559-5311. In the event of an emergency or if you need a minister after business hours, call 526-1766, extension 6, for the Pastor-of-the-Week on duty.

Using Church Facilities—All requests for the use of church facilities, excluding the Sanctuary and Wynne Chapel, should be directed to Mr. D. A. Sharpe, the church business manager through the reservation's secretary in the Business Office. Any proposed use of the church facilities, other than regularly assigned office space, should be scheduled as early as possible by a staff person from the department sponsoring the event.

Seating Capacity for most frequently used church facilities are: Sanctuary, 1,100; Wynne Chapel, 150; Elliott Fellowship Hall, 700 for seating and 500 for food service.

Ticket Sales are forbidden* by church policy, to any function held in the church or elsewhere, except where such tickets constitute costs of a meal held in the church. Groups and individuals are requested to refrain from promoting the sale of tickets or other admission tokens. *Exceptions are rarely made by the Session's Program Planning and Budgeting Council.

Weddings—The Sanctuary and Wynne Chapel are available for formal weddings only to members of Highland Park Presbyterian Church and members of other Presbyterian churches. One minister of this church shall officiate at all weddings, but he may invite any other minister to assist. Ms. Mary Lou Crow, wedding coordinator, is responsible for seeing that instructions for preparation for weddings, instructions to florists, and regulations regarding wedding receptions are carried out, except where the responsibility lies with the officiating minister.

Funerals—Requests for the services of any minister for a funeral should be referred to the minister desired, or to his secretary. All requests for using the Sanctuary or Wynne Chapel for funeral or memorial services should be cleared through the office of the secretary of the minister conducting the service, and the reservation's secretary in the Business Office should be notified.

Flowers in the Sanctuary are provided on most Sundays by various members. Generally, the flowers in the Sanctuary and Wynne Chapel are under the supervision of the Flower Committee of the Presbyterian Women. After use, flowers are disposed of as follows: Donor is encouraged to take them home or to shut-in friends. Food Service Director may use them for table decorations in Elliott Fellowship Hall.

Church Budget Pledges—Systematic and regular giving is encouraged by the church through pledges which are payable weekly, monthly, quarterly, semi-annually, or annually. While the church does not attempt to designate a particular method of paying a pledge, members should understand that expenses continue from day-to-day and week-to-week and bills must be paid at least monthly instead of quarterly. Most pledges are made on a family basis, but the church encourages all members of the family, who belong to the church, to feel a responsibility for a share in paying the pledge. Children are encouraged to have individual pledges, as a stewardship education value. Statements are rendered on pledges quarterly, unless a specific request is made for statements to be withheld. The church budget is prepared from April to August for the following calendar year and submitted to the session for approval and to the congregation for information.

Memorials, Endowments, Stock, and Trust Funds—Inquiries should be directed to Mr. D. A. Sharpe, the church business manager, or to the Highland Park Presbyterian Church Foundation.

Mailing Lists—A number of printed items are mailed on regular church mailing lists. These include Sunday bulletins, printed sermons, "The Highland Park Presbyterian WEEKLY," and promotional materials. New members are automatically added to this list, unless otherwise directed.